OUR
INCREDIBLE
CIVIL WAR

BOOKS BY *Burke Davis:*

WHISPER MY NAME
THE RAGGED ONES
YORKTOWN
THEY CALLED HIM STONEWALL
GRAY FOX
JEB STUART, THE LAST CAVALIER
TO APPOMATTOX
OUR INCREDIBLE CIVIL WAR

For Children:

ROBERTA E. LEE

OUR INCREDIBLE CIVIL WAR

---

by **Burke Davis**

DRAWINGS BY *Raymond Houhlihan*

HOLT, RINEHART AND WINSTON
NEW YORK

FIRST EDITION

LIBRARY OF CONGRESS CATALOG CARD NUMBER: 60-8192

81749–0510

PRINTED IN THE UNITED STATES OF AMERICA

ACKNOWLEDGMENT

THIS book was proposed by M.H. Elliott of High Point, North Carolina. Its scope was expanded by suggestions of Colonel John M. Virden, of Washington, D.C.; and by my North Carolina friends, Archie K. Davis of Winston-Salem, James Stedman, Fred Thompson, and A. Earl Weatherly of Greensboro; Charles R. Sanders, Jr., and Judge R. Hunt Parker of Raleigh; and John R. Peacock and Jacque White of High Point.

I am indebted to these compatriots, and to many who aided in the search for material, including especially:

Ralph G. Newman of Chicago, for use of a Nathan Bedford Forrest letter from his collection, and Richard B. Harwell of Chicago, for advice on sources.

Richard Steiner of Baltimore, for use of papers of his grandfather, Dr. Lewis Steiner, bearing on the Barbara Fritchie incident.

Van Dyk MacBride of Newark, New Jersey, for information on Confederate stamps, money, and the Great Seal of the Confederacy.

Neill Bohlinger of Little Rock, Arkansas, for colorful battle stories and lore.

T.W. Crigler, Jr., of Macon, Mississippi, for information on names of the war, stamps, money, and varied subjects.

Robert H. Bolton, of Alexandria, Louisiana, for aid in tracing facts on the first Confederate submarine, *Pioneer*.

Rear Admiral R. Bentham Simons, USN, Ret., of Charleston, South Carolina, for information on the submarine CSS *Hunley*.

Manuscript Division, Duke University Library, for use of a letter from General Peter B. Starke to Jefferson Davis.

James I. Robertson, Jr., editor of *Civil War History*, for a story of his great-grandfather, General R.E. Lee's cook.

Hubert A. Gurney, of Appomattox Court House National Military Park, Appomattox, Virginia, for details on the McLean House.

Miss Elizabeth Moore of New Bern, North Carolina, for information on Generals Gabriel and George Rains, CSA.

Charles J. Affleck, Winchester, Virginia, for information on Confederate currency, and operations in the Winchester area.

Hallie C. Turberville of Milton, North Carolina, for a story of the imprisonment of a relative, and of Sidney Lanier's days in prison.

Dr. E.R. MacLennan of Opp, Alabama, for an interesting diagnosis of the ailments of Stonewall Jackson.

Dr. T.W. Schmidt, of the Office of Ordnance Research, USA, for consultation on the problem of "The Confederate Satellite."

Commander Christopher A. Russell, USNR, Ret., of Baltimore, for stories of his grandfather and father, Major General C.C. Augur, USA, and Major George B. Russell, USA.

Brigadier General Frederick A. Stevens, USMC Res., Ret., of Melrose, Massachusetts, for letters and documents concerning his grandfather, Major Atherton H. Stevens, Jr.

Jacob M. Sheads of Gettysburg, Pennsylvania, for use of papers on John Burns prepared by his students, especially by Mary Lou Rhodes.

Virgil Carrington Jones of Washington, D.C., for information on Jefferson Davis in little-known sources, and for general advice.

Dr. North Callahan of Bronxville, New York, for information on descendants of famed Civil War figures.

John C. Pemberton III of New York for aid in tracing descendants.

Barbara Sweeny of the John G. Johnson Art Collection, Philadelphia, for information on the Manet painting of the battle between the *Kearsarge* and *Alabama*.

Rt. Hon. Arthur Henderson, Q.C., M.P., of London, for information on a descendant of John Breckinridge, and for other courtesies.

William F. Spivey, Superintendent, Fort McPherson National Cemetery, Maxwell, Nebraska, for information on the burial of Moses Milner, "alias Stonewall Jackson."

Miss Mary Elizabeth Sergent of Middletown, New York, for a musical program of Jeb Stuart's.

Mrs. Minnie Ransom Norris of Raleigh, North Carolina, for Confederate pension and other records.

Henry Maclin III of Greensboro, North Carolina, for records of Virginia Military Institute.

Dr. John Southworth of Greensboro, North Carolina, for material on the North-South Skirmish Association.

James Brawley of Salisbury, North Carolina, for information on a Confederate prisoner.

Nip Warriner and Dr. William H. Stauffer of Richmond, Virginia, for aid on Confederate arms and Virginia battlefield sites.

Miss Irene Hester of Greensboro Public Library.

Miss Jean Crawford of Holt, Rinehart and Winston, my invaluable editor.

My wife, Evangeline, my children, Angela and Burke, and the late Brunnhilde McIntyre, whose companionship and understanding make possible my labors.

BURKE DAVIS

TO
PHILLIPS RUSSELL
AND
WALTER SPEARMAN,
AND TO THE MEMORY OF
OSCAR JACKSON COFFIN

Why the Boom?

I HAVE a bulging file of letters from people who are, one way and another, entranced by the Civil War. I think of these as testimonials that the Boom will not collapse in our time.

There is one letter from former President Harry Truman, gently scolding me for my "solecistic" reference to General Robert E. Lee simply as "Robert Lee." Mr. Truman added, reasonably enough, that since our genuine heroes are so rare, their reputations should be guarded—an underlying theme in the creation of his great library in Missouri.

There is a letter from a young police officer in distant Leeds, Yorkshire, the father of five children, who is obsessed with the dream of visiting America for the single purpose of walking the Virginia battlefields of which he has read so much.

Mac Hyman, author of *No Time for Sergeants*, wrote that he was almost in tears at the end of my biography of Lee, ending with a deep-Georgia flourish: "Every time I read a book about that war, I have the far-off hope that maybe this time, just this one time, we will win it."

In this file, which could be matched by many a writer in the field of the American Civil War, are a few letters of outrage and condemnation. Stonewall Jackson's granddaughter upbraided me for writing what she thought a caricature of the great general. An elderly woman historian who had known many Confederate generals in her youth challenged me for having titled a book on Lee *Gray Fox*. A Virginia woman assailed me as "non-Southern" because of my account of the burning of Richmond by Confederates in *To Appomattox*—before reading the book. In her broadside she lumped me with the Soviet Union, the United States Supreme Court and Certain Republican Presidents fore and aft.

On the other hand, a New Yorker charged me with hero worship of Lee and more: "Over-emphasis upon the Christianity of the butcher in a human slaughter business by one who was a parasitic blueblood all his life." This one is filed under "Views of the War, Marxist."

Most of these correspondents ask information—on ancestors, old books, guns, stamps, money, uniforms, and the like. Some send manuscripts, diaries, and documents in bewildering variety. A Washington librarian offered an autograph book signed by J.E.B. Stuart, and a beech leaf he had plucked as a souvenir on his raid into Pennsylvania. A woman from New York State provided a copy of a missing musical program sung by Stuart and his staff for young ladies during the war.

A New York City physician, moved by an account of R.E. Lee's acquisition of his famed gray, Traveller, founded a movement to erect a monument on the spot, in Pocatelico, South Carolina.

A Swede wrote of his fascination with our war after reading *To Appomattox*, but said that the adversaries were so much alike in outlook, background, and purpose, that he wondered why they had fought.

Many letters offer stories unknown to history.

One woman wrote of her aunt, whose husband was in Lincoln's Cabinet, and of her spirited foray across the Potomac with the vanguard of the Union Army to rescue the furniture and equipment of Arlington, the Lee House. This vigorous woman, a friend of the Lee family, routed vandals, directed the gathering of broken fragments of "The Cincinnati" dinner set from the Arlington lawn, and saw to it that household goods were stored for postwar return to the Lees.

A retired naval officer sent details of the role played by his grandfather in escorting to a Boston prison the Confederate generals captured just before Appomattox—including a new, touching account of General R.S. Ewell bursting into sobs when he learned of Lincoln's death. The same young officer presided over the hanging of Henry Wirz, the Andersonville jailer; copies of original documents supported this interesting letter.

A surprising number of pro-Confederate messages come from the North and Midwest. A sixteen-year-old Pennsylvania boy: "Though I am a native of Gettysburg, I am a Johnny Reb in word, thought and deed." A young man from Warren, Ohio: "My only regret is that I was not born a Southerner."

In general, though the letters are neither sectional nor partisan, they reveal an intense, almost evangelical, concern with the subject.

I believe that these people, like thousands drawn to the Civil War, could not define the reasons for their intense interest. Perhaps the lure is not, as is so often claimed, that this was "The Most American War," or "The Last Medieval and the First Modern War." Perhaps it is simply because the conflict was so astonishingly rich and varied that it is inexhaustible. More than one hundred thousand volumes of its literature thus far have failed to tell the tale to the satisfaction of today's readers.

Those who begin with the notion that the war took place in Virginia discover that there were more than 5,500 actions about 95 of them real battles—and that California saw six skirmishes, New Mexico nineteen, Oregon four, with others in Utah, Idaho, and Washington Territory. Land fighting may be traced as far north as St. Albans, Vermont, where there was a Confederate raid; other raiders struck in New York, Illinois, and Minnesota.

The final action of the war was at the edge of the Arctic Circle. The southernmost sweep of the Union blockade was to a lonely sand spur on the Florida coast destined for later fame: Cape Canaveral.

This book is a sampler of some of my favorite tales, facts, coincidences, and oddities of the strange, romantic, brutal conflict from which the modern United States emerged.

It was written for those who are already hobbyists and for those who wonder what all the shouting is about. It was assembled in years of reading for other purposes, sometimes aimless, but disciplined by constant noting and filing. It is by no means all-inclusive.

Only two bits have been deleted on the ground of Unsuitability For Family Reading—both from the section called "Sex in the War." One was a rendition of a bawdy ballad inspired by Confederate ordnance men who collected homely ingredients for their gunpowder factories from family chamber pots. The other was an account of Jefferson Davis and an alleged escapade with a woman friend on a Pullman car, postwar. Enterprising searchers for Truth and Beauty (or that brand offered by the press) will find some hilarious paragraphs in the Washington *Star* of July 18, or the Louisville *Commercial* of July 15, of the year 1871. The author will fill no requests for copies of this Confederate *erotica curiosa*.

The range of the book is great, from the strictly factual bulk of it (as nearly as can be determined after almost a century) to half legend, pure legend—and even high fantasy. No documentation of the usual sort has been attempted, but stray scholars will note that much material is drawn from sources familiar to them, though not to the average reader. Some of it appears here in print for the first time.

In my youth there was little interest in the Civil War among boys. Today, the country seems abruptly filled with young Civil War buffs. Much of my correspondence has been with them; they bring refreshing ideas to the study of the time.

Much of this book was written with the "new crop" of American Civil War enthusiasts in mind, in the hope that it might lead some to serious study of this dark but wonderful time in our history.

BURKE DAVIS

Williamsburg, Virginia
March 28, 1960

Contents

OUR
INCREDIBLE
CIVIL WAR

1

The Travail of Wilmer McLean

MAJOR WILMER McLEAN might well have said, as tradition has it, "The war began in my front yard and ended in my parlor."

McLean, a well-to-do wholesale grocer from Alexandria, had retired in 1854 to a pleasant estate along Bull Run, near Manassas Junction, in Prince William County, Virginia. He had made many improvements on the plantation, including a massive stone barn.

The place was known as "Yorkshire," for the home county of a previous owner, Colonel Richard Blackburn, a migrant Englishman.

Roads in the neighborhood led to the nearby rail line and important villages, and several crossed Bull Run not far from the farmhouse. One of these crossings was McLean's Ford.

In May, 1861, the line of Bull Run was occupied by Confederate troops to guard against an expected Federal thrust from Washington. Many regiments camped on or near Yorkshire, and Camp Wigfall was established on its southernmost acres.

Just behind McLean's Ford, and on either side, General J.R. Jones had his brigade raise earthworks which remain today—though much reduced by bulldozers—amid a housing development known as Yorkshire Village.

On July 18, when Federals approached the site, General P.G.T. Beauregard, the Confederate commander, left his headquarters at a nearby farmhouse and went to Yorkshire. The general was riding the front lines at noon of that day when a Union shell dropped into a chimney of the McLean house, fell into the kitchen fireplace, and immediately exploded in a kettle of stew.

The stew was splattered over the room and the luncheon menu for the general, his staff, and the McLean household was revised.

The action in which this shot was fired threw General Daniel Tyler's Federal division against General James Longstreet's Confederates—a skirmish known to Confederates as the Battle of Bull Run, as opposed to the larger engagement of July 21 (which they called the Battle of Manassas, but the Federals called Bull Run).

Casualties from this fight were placed in Major McLean's big barn, but officers were forced to move them when Union gunners shelled the place. Beauregard commented bitterly on enemy treatment of the McLean barn, saying that it was "surmounted by the usual yellow hospital flag. I hope, for the sake of past associations, that it was ignorantly mistaken for a Confederate flag."

Beauregard stayed at Yorkshire for three days while troops maneuvered over the farm.

McLean had had enough of war, and when the armies had gone, he bought a farm in isolated southern Virginia, its red brick house fronting a street in the village of Appomattox Courthouse. The McLean family seems to have lived peacefully for three years in their new home. Back at Yorkshire, the armies crossed Bull Run and the familiar fields in the Second Manassas campaign. And, in October of 1863, Jeb Stuart's artillery fought a day's engagement on the farm as part of Lee's withdrawal after Gettysburg.

The war caught up with Wilmer McLean about noon of Sunday, April 9, 1865. The major was walking in the village street, probably alarmed at the number of Confederate troops lying near his home, now that the early-morning fire had ceased.

A young officer in a worn gray uniform hailed him, asking for a place where General Lee might meet with General Grant.

McLean showed the officer—Colonel Charles Marshall—an unoccupied brick building in the center of the village. Lee's aide looked into its unfurnished interior and declined it: "Isn't there some other place?"

McLean took him to his home just west of the courthouse, its lawn shaded by trees, its white picket fence sagging—probably the result of the morning's action.

Marshall followed McLean into the parlor and approved. The colonel recalled in his memoirs that Colonel Orville Babcock of Grant's staff went in with them to wait for the meeting of commanders: "So General Lee, Babcock and myself sat down in McLean's parlor and talked in the most friendly and affable way."

By 4 P.M. it was all over. Lee and Grant rode away—and the looting of the house began. The McLean family was besieged by offers from Federals to buy souvenirs. Many pressed greenbacks upon Major McLean, who protested that he did not wish to sell.

General Sheridan "bought" the table on which surrender terms were written, and donated it to the wife of General Custer; it is now in the Smithsonian Institution. General Ord got the table upon which Grant and Lee signed the terms, and it is today at the Chicago Historical Society.

Some officers, chiefly of cavalry, tried to buy chairs used by Lee and Grant, and when they were refused, took them off on horseback. Chairs with cane bottoms were cut up for mementoes, and the strips of cane handed out to Federals in the yard. Upholstery was cut to ribbons.

Sylvanus Cadwallader, the New York *Herald* correspondent, was in the crowd. He made a quick sketch of the McLean House, of which copies were sent North, some to be published, others to be reproduced and sold for the benefit of old soldiers.

The McLean House stood until 1893, when it was carefully dismantled for removal to Washington for an exhibition. The financiers of the project were ruined in the panic of that year, and the materials were never reassembled. Timbers, bricks, doors, and windows lay in the open until they deteriorated beyond repair.

The contractor who tore down the house, C.W. Hancock of Lynchburg, was not paid for his work because of the bankruptcy of the promoters.

A facsimile of the house was made possible for posterity by

one P.C. Hubard, who made detailed drawings for Hancock, a copy of which was preserved in a Lynchburg library.

In 1948 the Federal Government ordered the McLean House rebuilt in an exact replica of the original, using the Hubard drawings. The contractor chosen for the work was E.H. Hancock, the youngest son of the demolisher. The price of the restoration was $49,553.

The State of Virginia appropriated five thousand dollars toward furnishings. Donations in cash and furniture came from many private sources, and in 1950, in the presence of U.S. Grant III and Robert E. Lee IV, the house was dedicated as part of the national park in the courthouse village.

In 1960 the only piece of original furniture in the surrender parlor of the house was a horsehair sofa purchased from a granddaughter of Major McLean.

Reproductions of the chairs and tables used by Lee and Grant were on display, copied from the originals at the Chicago Historical Society and the Smithsonian Institution.

Other original items, including furniture, jewelry, silver, and utensils, are in the house, gifts of other McLean descendants.

2

House Divided

AMERICA was a house of brothers weirdly divided when catastrophe struck in 1861.

The White House was the leading example of the schism. Four of Lincoln's brothers-in-law wore Confederate uniforms and one of them, Lieutenant David P. Todd, was charged with brutality to Union prisoners in Richmond.

Mary Lincoln's brother, Dr. George R.C. Todd, was a volunteer Confederate surgeon, and was quoted as saying that Lincoln was "one of the greatest scoundrels unhung."

Ben Hardin Helm, killed as a Confederate general at Chickamauga, was married to one of Mary Lincoln's sisters; he had spurned a personal offer of a commission from Lincoln. Mary's other two sisters were also married to Confederate officers.

Washington gossip spoke of Mrs. Lincoln as "two-thirds pro-slavery and the other third Secesh."

The Lincolns' troubles on this score came to a head when Senate members of the Committee on the Conduct of the War met to consider charges of treason against Mary. Lincoln made a surprise appearance to read a brief statement denying that any member of his family had treated with the enemy.

Thousands of men switched sides during the war, usually by desertion, but in at least two well-authenticated cases, soldiers fought formally on both sides, resigning in order to change uniforms.

Captain Frank C. Armstrong of the 2nd U.S. Cavalry fought in blue at First Manassas, or Bull Run, resigned the following month and went South to become a Confederate brigadier general.

His companion in arms, Lieutenant Manning M. Kimmel, also fought with the 2nd Cavalry in the first major battle of the war, resigned soon after Armstrong, and became Assistant Adjutant General to the Confederate General Earl Van Dorn. Lieutenant Kimmel became the father of Admiral Husband E. Kimmel, who was in command at Pearl Harbor, December 7, 1941.

Old Henry Clay's grandsons were soldiers, three for the Union, four for the Confederacy.

Senator George B. Crittenden of Kentucky was proud of two sons who became major generals, one on each side.

James W. Ripley, the Federal chief of ordnance, had a fire-breathing nephew, General Roswell Ripley, who fought in gray.

At Bull Run Frederick Hubbard of the Washington Artillery of New Orleans, who wore gray, for the first time in seven years met Henry Hubbard of the 1st Minnesota infantry, who wore blue. The brothers were wounded, and by coincidence placed side by side in the stable which served as a hospital.

Colonel John S. Mosby, the Confederate Ranger, slipped into Alexandria and captured Colonel D.H. Dulaney, USA. He had a well-qualified guide in his ranks, French Dulaney, the son of his victim.

Jeb Stuart's chief of staff, Major H.B. McClellan, had four brothers in blue and a first cousin, George B. McClellan, was twice commander of the Army of the Potomac.

General Philip St. George Cooke, USA, had three daughters who married generals, one with the Union, two Confederate. One of the latter was Mrs. Jeb Stuart. Cooke's son, John, became a Southern general, and did not speak to his father for several years after the war. When Jeb Stuart made his most famous ride, around a big Union army, he galloped through a sector where his father-in-law was in command.

The war was touched off by an artillery duel between Confederates ashore at Charleston, South Carolina, and a garrison of Federal troops at Fort Sumter in the harbor. Commander of the handful in blue was Major Robert Anderson, whose father-in-law was a Governor of Georgia. Anderson had been so adept as an artillery pupil in his days at West Point that his instructor had broken tradition to keep him as an assistant. The Confederate commander who directed firing on Sumter was the instructor himself, General P.G.T. Beauregard.

Stonewall Jackson was the symbol of Southern resistance, but his sister Laura, a Union sympathizer, remained unshaken in her devotion to the Old Republic, and was applauded for her stand by Federal soldiers. She sent a message by a Union soldier to the effect that she could "take care of wounded Federals as fast as brother Thomas would wound them."

Albert T. Bledsoe, a West Pointer, Episcopal clergyman and lawyer, had made his office next door to Lincoln's in Springfield, Illinois. Bledsoe became Assistant Secretary of War, Confederate States.

It was Lincoln's law partner, John Todd Stuart, who landed a West Point berth for a young soldier of promise, George E. Pickett, whose name became so inseparably linked with Gettysburg.

Captain Samuel Barron was made head of a Navy bureau by Lincoln in April of 1861—when five days earlier he had accepted a commission as a Confederate commodore. Barron soon went South to command forts in the Carolinas and Virginia.

An intricate case of divided loyalties involved John C. Pemberton, a Pennsylvania Quaker who had two brothers in the

U.S. cavalry, but became the Confederate general in charge of Vicksburg's defenses. Pemberton married a woman from Norfolk, Virginia—one of whose in-laws was a Tennessee-born naval officer, David G. Farragut, who became the first admiral of the U.S. Navy. When Pemberton was penned in Vicksburg, Farragut's victories below him on the Mississippi helped to seal his doom.

Though Farragut was born of a North Carolina mother and reared in New Orleans and Virginia, he did not hesitate to choose the Union.

A final bit of irony for General Pemberton lay in the flotilla of gunboats which ran his gantlet of guns at Vicksburg and helped to defeat him. The boats were commanded by Alexander M. Pennock, who was married to another of his wife's sisters.

Distorted echoes of these divisions came to Pemberton when he surrendered Vicksburg to U.S. Grant on July 4, 1863. Southern partisans accused him of masquerading as a Confederate, and of cruel betrayal by giving up the city on the national holiday. Pemberton's reply: "I am a Northern man. I know my people. . . . I know we can get better terms from them on the 4th of July than any other day of the year."

Federal guards picked up a pretty girl who was smuggling quinine through the lines to Rebels in Fauquier County, Virginia, carrying the precious medicine sewn into her skirts. She landed in Washington's Old Capitol Prison, but emerged when she was discovered to be Louisa P. Buckner, niece of the Postmaster General of the United States, Montgomery Blair.

In Confederate eyes General Ben Butler, "The Beast of New Orleans," was perhaps the most despicable enemy figure, yet Butler had been a proslavery Democrat, and it was he who had once tried to nominate Jefferson Davis for the Presidency of the United States, a move which, if successful, might have averted war.

Commodore Franklin Buchanan, first head of the United States Naval Academy, went South to command the old *Mer-*

rimac when she became the ironclad *Virginia*. One of Buchanan's battle victims was the USS *Congress*, on which his brother was an officer.

In 1859, when the *Merrimac* was new, and a pride of the United States fleet, Senator Stephen Mallory of Florida led an inspection party as chairman of the Senate's Naval Affairs Committee. Two years later, in his role as Confederate Secretary of Navy, he made her a pioneer ironclad.

For the siege of Vicksburg, Missouri furnished thirty-nine regiments—seventeen Confederate, twenty-two Union.

The climax of the war for the 7th Tennessee Regiment, Confederate, was the capture of the complete 7th Tennessee, USA—warriors, drummers, cooks, and all.

During the battle of Gettysburg John Wentz, an eighty-seven-year-old farmer, hid in the cellar of his home while, in the yard above, his son, whom he had not seen for twenty-four years, fought in gray with the Washington Artillery of New Orleans. By tradition, the younger Wentz entered the cellar, found his father sleeping, and left a note pinned to his coat.

Not far away, on the same landscape, was another divided Pennsylvania family. John Culp, owner of Culp's Hill, had one son in gray and one in blue. Both took part in the bitter fighting for the slopes of the homeplace.

Confederates captured Galveston, Texas, shelling and seizing the USS *Harriet Lane*. Major A.M. Lea went aboard the vessel with a boarding party. He found on deck, in dying condition, a lieutenant of the *Lane*, his son.

When a Federal fleet captured Port Royal, South Carolina, the commander of defenses was Confederate General Thomas F. Drayton. A captain on one of the attacking ships, the USS *Pocahontas*, was Drayton's brother.

General Armistead L. Long, of Robert E. Lee's staff, was a son-in-law of the Federal corps commander, General Edwin V. Sumner.

General Patrick Cleburne, CSA, had one brother in the Southern army and one in the Northern.

Francis Lieber, the famed political scientist, adviser to the United States on military and international law during the war, had two sons in blue, and another killed in gray.

Captain John L. Inglis, an Englishman with the Confederacy, led his Florida company on a valiant charge, overran the Federal guns, and accepted the surrender of their commander, his brother.

The troops of these strangely divided armies were taught tactics from the same book, written by a Confederate, General W.J. Hardee.

3

Firsts

AS the breeding ground for modern warfare, the Civil War has long been known for its "firsts." It has been credited with dozens like these:

Railroad artillery
A successful submarine
A "snorkel" breathing device
The periscope, for trench warfare
Land-mine fields
Field trenches on a grand scale
Flame throwers
Wire entanglements
Military telegraph
Naval torpedoes
Aerial reconnaissance
Antiaircraft fire
Repeating rifles
Telescopic sights for rifles
Long-range rifles for general use
Fixed ammunition
Ironclad navies
A steel ship
Revolving gun turrets
Military railroads
Organized medical and nursing corps
Hospital ships
Army ambulance corps
A workable machine gun

Legal voting for servicemen
U.S. Secret Service
The income tax
Withholding tax
Tobacco tax
Cigarette tax
American conscription
American bread lines
The Medal of Honor
A wide-ranging corps of press correspondents in battle
    areas
Photography of battle
The bugle call, "Taps"
Negro U.S. Army officer (Major M.R. Delany)

American President assassinated
Department of Justice (Confederate)
Commissioned American Army chaplains
U.S. Navy admiral
Electrically exploded bombs and torpedoes
The wigwag signal code in battle
Wide-scale use of anesthetics for wounded
Blackouts and camouflage under aerial observation

The first organized aerial psychological warfare was the
dropping of Lincoln's Amnesty Proclamation behind Southern
lines by the use of kites, a technique used experimentally in the
Napoleonic Wars.

The first naval camouflage was used by the mist-gray
blockade runners.

The first smoke screen was used by the *R.E. Lee*, running the blockade and escaping the USS *Iroquois*.

A gun battery propelled by an armored locomotive in Federal Service was the precursor of both the tank and the self-propelled gun.

The first "aircraft carrier" was a boat designed especially for hauling balloons.

The first flares for marksmen shooting at night were calcium lights developed by a Major Edge, of Berdan's Sharpshooters, a famous Federal regiment.

The first "economic warfare" was used by the North in massive counterfeiting of Confederate currency. Union printers flooded the South with this bogus money, its only defect being its superiority to the genuine article; printers went so far as to duplicate five-cent notes of Confederate towns and business enterprises, as a spur to inflation.

Not every first can be pinpointed with conclusive evidence, but stout claims have been made for these and more.

Despite the modern developments spawned by the war, thousands of men went into the early fighting in body armor, assured by newspaper advertisements that iron breastplates would shield them from death. Heavy casualties attested to the tragic inefficiency of the gear.

Many inventions pouring into the warring capitals bordered on lunacy, but some forecast the future.

Simeon Draper of New York proposed to scoffing ordnance officers a balloon shell like those used by Japan against the American Northwest in World War II. A Federal balloonist went aloft with grenades and bombs, with the bottom of his wicker carriage shielded against ground fire by an iron plate. And one inventor tried in vain to interest the United States in a rocket-driven torpedo which behaved like a guided missile in its tests.

Both Union and Confederate inventors turned out weird forked-barrel cannon, designed to fire two shot simultaneously, joined by chains, so that enemy troops would be mowed down if they stood in a convenient place.

Confederates built a steam-powered cannon of mammoth size which flung balls from a hopper without benefit of gunpowder, but too many shot merely trickled from the barrel.

The Federal armies were offered a miraculous water-walking device which would make military bridges a thing of the past—each soldier would wear tiny canoes on his feet, and drive himself over the water with a small paddle.

4

The First Battle

IN June, 1861, Confederate troops dug trenches in the sandy lowlands where Virginia's history had begun, between Jamestown and Yorktown. The enemy was not far away, at Fortress Monroe. The workmen found relics of the Revolution and the surrender of Cornwallis, but, until the sixth of June, war seemed far away.

The Southern commander was Prince John Magruder, late artillery major in the United States Army, of whom army gossips said that he had come here pouting, having been refused a Federal command of his choice. One of his lieutenants was Daniel H. Hill, a tart-tongued North Carolinian, and a colonel of the 1st North Carolina Volunteers, who was brother-in-law to Thomas J. Jackson, a professor at Virginia Military Institute.

On June 6, Hill pushed his untrained troops toward battle. Their goal was Bethel Church, a settlement evacuated by the enemy, where Yankees had scrawled on church walls "Death to the traitors!" and "Down with the Rebels!"

The regiment was all day marching the thirteen miles from Yorktown to Big Bethel Church and the men were worn out at dusk, still in heavy marching order, burdened with knapsacks, canteens, loaded cartridge boxes, extra shoes and tin cups dangling, and Bibles in many a pack. In a drizzling rain the troops cooked their first meal in the field, on ramrods, and slept without tents.

There was a grove of pines about the unpainted country church, from which the land fell away to the south and on both sides of the roadway; behind the church was a ravine and a creek. Little more than a hundred yards from the church a wooden bridge spanned the creek. Hill placed artillery to cover the bridge.

The regiment had only twenty-five spades, six axes and three picks, but they were kept busy day and night, and by June 8 the churchyard looked like a fort. Hill sent out one company that afternoon to chase off some Federals who were plundering a house.

On the same afternoon another of Hill's companies saw their first American flags in battle, near a Federal camp at Hampton. The green Confederate troops rashly charged almost to the gates of the camp, driving a bluecoat band into the bivouac.

Colonel Hill feared that this would bring on an engagement; civilians reported that the Yankees had taken away dead and wounded in two carts and a buggy. There were no Confederate casualties.

These may have been the first Federal battle casualties; more were to come within two days.

At 3 A.M., June 10, Colonel Hill sent his regiment against the enemy, but when they learned that Federals were ahead of them in strength they "fell hastily back" to their trenches.

There was a long wait. Officers of the Confederate regiment made up a purse for an old woman of the neighborhood who had warned them of the enemy's presence. They collected $225.

A fury of firing swept the scene at daybreak, for most of the troops at Bethel the first such sounds of the war.

General Benjamin Butler had sent seven Federal regiments to surround and capture Hill's Confederates at Bethel, but in the darkness two of these had collided, firing on each other, leaving nineteen wounded and two dead. Other Federal commanders came to the scene of this firing and held a council of war in the field. They decided to call for reinforcements and wade in on the position at Bethel—4,400 Federals against 1,408 Confederate defenders.

Private Edward Hale of the 1st North Carolina watched the enemy come:

At nine o'clock the head of the enemy's column [Bendix' 7th New York] appeared in the road, half a mile away, and soon they seemed to fill it. Who will forget that tremendous moment, ushering in the war! A few minutes after nine o'clock a shot from Randolph's Parrott gun screamed away at them. It hit the earth just in their front and ricocheted. They fell away from the road like a mist before the sun, their artillery at once replied, and the battle began.

The bluecoats stabbed at Hill's right, but were broken by the ravine and creek and driven off by artillery. There were tentative charges and countercharges, one of them pressed hard by the Confederates with the valor of ignorance. Even yet, Hill had not lost a man.

For twenty minutes the Federals hammered at Hill's left, and were driven off by a heavy fire which killed a Union major, Theodore Winthrop. Claimants for the honor of inflicting this casualty were three of Hill's privates and the Negro body servant of a fourth—the latter a crack shot. At noon the battle dwindled, and Colonel Hill sent five volunteers on a mission which did not seem dangerous to the untrained soldiers. This party was to burn a farmhouse which had been used by sharpshooters of both sides.

Private John Thorpe, who ran into the open with this group, described the first Confederate battle casualty of the war:

I saw a Zouave regiment of the enemy in line of battle about 300 yards away. Our boys popped away at them . . . they marched away down the New Market road.

A few minutes later Colonel Hill said, "Captain Bridgers, can't you have that house burned?" Captain Bridgers asked if five of the company would volunteer to burn it, suggesting that one of the number should be an officer. Corp. George T. Williams said he would be the officer and four others said they would go. Matches and a hatchet were provided at once, and a minute later the little party scrambled over the breastworks in the following order:

George Williams, Thomas Fallon, John Thorpe, Henry Wyatt and R.H. Bradley.

A volley was fired at us as if by a company, not from the house, but from the road to our left. As we were well drilled in skirmishing, all of us instantly dropped to the ground, Wyatt mortally wounded.

He never uttered a word or a groan, but lay limp on his back, his arms extended, one knee up and a clot of blood on his forehead as large as a man's fist. He was lying within four feet of me and this is the way I saw him. . . . To look at Wyatt one would take him to be tenacious of life; low, but robust in build, guileless, open, frank, aggressive.

Wyatt died during the night in Yorktown, and his body went to Richmond for burial, the first of thousands to be conducted in that city for battle casualties. Camps were named for Wyatt, and the loss of the twenty-year-old boy became part of the rallying cry for troops from North Carolina: "First at Bethel, Farthest at Gettysburg, Last at Appomattox."

The Bethel skirmish touched off delirious joy in the South. The Charleston *Courier* cried:

We learn that a great reaction has taken place among the moneyed men of New York and Boston, and that petitions are now circulating to be laid before Congress, asking the peaceful recognition of the Southern Confederacy and the establishment of amicable relations. . . . The petitions set forth that unless the war is brought to a close very speedily New York and Boston are ruined cities.

The Richmond *Dispatch:*

It is one of the most extraordinary victories in the annals of war. Four thousand thoroughly drilled and equipped troops routed and driven from the field by only eleven hundred men. Two hundred of the enemy killed, and on our side but one life lost. Does not the hand of God seem manifest in this thing?

Overnight, D.H. Hill was a brigadier general.

5

Mr. Lincoln's Beard

LINCOLN was the sixteenth American President, and the first to wear a beard. He set so enduring a precedent that, of the next nine men elected to the office after him, only William McKinley was clean-shaven.

The presidential candidate had apparently never given a thought to growing whiskers until, about October 18, 1860, he had a letter from eleven-year-old Grace Bedell of Westfield, New York, proposing that he give up shaving:

> I have got four brothers and part of them will vote for you any way and if you will let your whiskers grow I will try and get the rest of them to vote for you; you would look a great deal better for your face is so thin. . . . All the ladies like whiskers and they would tease their husbands to vote for you and then you would be President.

Lincoln replied the next day:

> . . . As to the whiskers, having never worn any, do you not think people would call it a piece of silly affectation if I were to begin it now?

Within a very few weeks Lincoln appeared unshaven, and stubble sprouted on his long chin. On November 26 he had his first bearded photograph made—a thin straggling line of dark hair along his jaws. On January 26, when he sat for his next photograph, the beard was still scraggly, and only by February 9, just before he left Springfield for Washington, had his beard

grown into the familiar appendage on the most famous face in
American history.

Lincoln's route from Illinois to Washington was long and
tortuous. He was two weeks on the way, halting at whistle stops
to be seen by curious people who stared at him as a symbol of
a new, strange and dangerous time.

One of the stops was at Westfield, New York, and here
Lincoln paused in his speech:

> During my campaign I had a little correspondent from
> your town. She kindly admonished me to let my whiskers
> grow, and since I've taken her advice, I would like to see
> her. Is she here? Is Grace Bedell here?

A little girl was handed up through the crowd, and Lincoln
kissed her while people applauded. Busy newspaper correspondents hurried the story away before the train left the station.

Lincoln did not please all who saw him in the new guise.
Not long after, when the President was inaugurated in Washington, his former law partner, William H. Herndon, kept a
bright-eyed watch:

> He was raising . . . a crop of whiskers of the
> blacking-brush variety, coarse, stiff and ungraceful; and
> in so doing he spoiled a face which, though never handsome,
> had in its original state a peculiar power and pathos.

6

The Blockade

WHEN Abraham Lincoln began to blockade the four thousand tortuous miles of Southern coastline, he had twenty-six steamers to cover a distance greater than the New York-Liverpool run. His entire navy had but sixty-nine ships, all wooden, half of them sailing vessels.

The Union finally built two hundred new steam vessels for the task, seventy-four of them ironclads, and spent millions in the first modern effort to strangle a nation by naval blockade. Historians still squabble over whether this brought the South to her knees—but, in any case, the blockade provided some of the most spectacular exploits of the war.

To the tune of outraged squeals of protest, Lincoln extended the blockade to the coasts of North Carolina and Virginia before they actually seceded from the Union.

Secretary of State Seward blundered in the original act by declaring Southern ports blockaded, rather than closed—a legal technicality that gave the Confederacy the status of a belligerent and opened the way to foreign adventurers and profiteers, chiefly British.

The Federal net caught only one of every ten blockade-runners in 1861, one of eight in 1862, one of four in 1863, and one of two in 1865. The average was about one out of every six.

Profits to the lucky ones were fantastic. Cotton could be bought for three cents a pound in the South, and fetched from

40 cents to a dollar in England. The profit on 1,000 bales of cotton, delivered by a fast steamer within two weeks, was about $250,000.

Captains earned up to $5,000 per trip, half in advance. The chief officer drew $1,250, the second and third mates $750, the chief engineer $2,500, the crew and firemen $250 each, the pilot, $3,500.

Skippers in the trade, especially British, made this toast famous during the war:

> Here's to the Confederates that grow the cotton, the Yanks that keep up the price by blockade, the Limeys that pay the high prices for it—to all three and a long war.

Statistics are many and unreliable, but a few may guide:

Some 66 vessels left England for the blockade trade during the war, and about 40 were captured or destroyed. Most of them paid investors well, making many voyages.

The total number of blockade-runners is estimated to have been as high as 1,650, averaging five successful trips each, carrying goods worth about two billion dollars.

Cotton carried to England was about 540,000 bales, with perhaps as much more smuggled illegally into the North. (Yankee traders were often guilty of breaking Lincoln's Blockade. A favorite trick was to buy cotton for eight cents per pound or less from Rebels in the South, get it across the lines as the property of foreign subjects who were exempt, or under forged bills of sale. It brought fancy prices in the North. One New Orleans Frenchman made $20,000 by agreeing to ship cotton as his own. A footnote to the lively smuggling trade: An Irishman whose mule died in the South profited by allowing the animal's carcass to be stuffed with quinine worth $10,000, and moved into Federal lines. On the other hand, enterprising Yankees unfettered by patriotic sentiments shipped pistols south from Boston in lard barrels.)

In the first half of 1861 the entire nail supply of the South was controlled by four or five Richmond speculators, who sent the price from $4 to $10 per keg.

Salt rose from 1 cent to 50 cents per pound. Iron rose from $25 per ton to $1,500.

The South was slow to move against this threat. It was 1864 before the cotton exchange plan went into effect, gaining credit in Europe when it was too late. The government also forcibly reserved space for army supplies on blockaders, at the expense of profiteers, but only the Confederate ordnance bureau and the State of North Carolina resorted to buying their own blockade-runners for public service. General Josiah Gorgas, the genius of the ordnance effort, bought four packets: *Cornelia, R.E. Lee, Merrimack,* and *Phantom,* which made more than fifty trips before August, 1863.

North Carolina's ship, *Advance,* made seven or eight successful trips.

Her chief engineer was James Maglenn, an Irishman who had voted for Lincoln and boasted of it, to the dismay of Southern patriots. This ship carried on her maiden voyage a French professor, J.J. Ayres, who went to Liverpool to buy textbook stereotypes for Edgeworth Female Seminary of Greensboro, North Carolina.

Arms were brought to the South in impressive quantities, so that Confederate troops were often better armed than their adversaries. The blockader *Fingal* brought in 7,500 Enfield rifles and 17,000 pounds of cannon powder in November, 1861.

In February, 1863, imports from Bermuda included about 80,000 Enfield rifles, 27,000 Austrian rifles, 2,100 British muskets, 2,000 Brunswick rifles, 354 carbines, 129 cannon.

(In the year beginning September, 1862, only 35,000 small arms were made in the South, and three or four times as many were smuggled in.)

Between November, 1863, and December, 1864, the runners brought in 8,500,000 pounds of meat and 500,000 pounds of coffee.

As the blockade system settled down to the grim process of attrition this routine was worked out by Southerners and their British allies: Big British steamers, loaded with arms and luxuries from Europe, unloaded at Bermuda or Nassau and took on cotton for their return. The last miles, slipping into Confederate ports, were covered by the swift, lean, light-draft ships designed for the service, all painted black or misty gray. About 200 of these were at work in the last phase of the war, all running familiar sea lanes. Bermuda to Wilmington, North Carolina, was the longest run—674 miles; it was 515 miles from Nassau into Charleston, and 500 to Savannah.

The trade was kept alive by Wilmington for the last two years. It was an ideal haven for smugglers, since the Federal fleet could not effectively block the mouth of the Cape Fear River, which was divided by an island and blocked by a shallow bar. Wilmington was a few miles upriver, and just at the entrance, dominating the spot with big guns until near the end of the war, was Fort Fisher. The gray steamers went in and out of this port, invisible more than a hundred yards away by night or in the fog, their engines unheard in the roar of breakers. Early in 1864 two thirds of the runs from the port were still successful, but by the end of the year 40 of 66 were caught.

In all, the Federals took 1,149 ships as prizes, in addition to the 355 burned or driven ashore. The total loss was about 1,500. Prize courts allowed over $22,000,000 in cargoes condemned, and by conservative estimates the vessels involved were worth $7,000,000.

Thirty blockade-runners were lost on a twelve-mile stretch of beach above the Cape Fear, and in 1960 many wrecks were visible in the surf at low tide—one of them at a fishing pier, a lure to skin divers.

Typical of the blockade-runners was *Banshee 11*, which made eight successful trips, and paid her owners a 700 per cent profit despite her capture. On one trip this little steamer brought in 600 barrels of pork and 1,500 boxes of meat, enough to supply Lee's army for a month.

In late December, 1864, the *Banshee* went on a round trip to Nassau, and her British skipper, Thomas Taylor, took on a cargo for $6,000, returning to Wilmington eighteen days later with a profit of $27,000.

On one such trip the *Banshee* almost met her fate when a white Arabian horse being imported from Egypt for Jefferson Davis neighed while the runner was slipping by the Federal fleet. The enemy opened fire, but the blockader escaped in darkness, eased over the bar, and sped up the river.

The *R.E. Lee*, of the little government fleet, made twenty-one round trips, carrying 7,000 bales of cotton worth some $2,000,000 in gold, and bringing in enough war supplies to pay for herself many times over.

7

Music, Music

AT the height of the battle of Shiloh, when the issue was much in doubt, a Federal band blared away at tunes from *Il Trovatore*, as thousands of blue-clad soldiers huddled under the river bluffs, and their comrades held off the Confederates.

Not long afterward, as the furious first day's fighting dragged to an end, a fresh regiment came ashore from its boats, with a band playing *"Hail Columbia."* Some officers thought it helped to save the day for the Union.

Robert E. Lee once listened to a band concert in camp and said, "I don't see how we could have an army without music."

Both armies applied music to problems of morale.

Federal armies in the first days of the war had half their regiments equipped with bands. Musicians drew higher pay than privates, and hats were passed for them after concerts; this attracted many famous civilian bands. Most Union bands were of twenty-two pieces, and they overcame Confederate competition in many engagements. Southern troops gathered eagerly to listen to music from enemy bands, throughout the war.

Fifty Union bands staged a Sunday concert at the White House before the Seven Days battles in 1862, but served only to arm critics in the North and reduce the blare of martial music. It was charged that the War Department spent $4,000,000 a year on bands, and that in July, 1862, there were 618 bands in service, a ratio of one musician to every forty-one soldiers. The protests ended regimental bands, and thereafter only brigades

had official bands—of sixteen men each. Best of them were the German bands, thoroughly trained in civilian life.

Most Confederate bands had but three or four pieces, usually played by Germans, and though they got no such handsome treatment as Federal musicians, the Southerners adapted themselves readily. Bandsmen learned to serenade the most prosperous-looking houses in a neighborhood, in return for food. The piano player would walk uninvited into the house, play at the instrument until the family gathered, and charm the hosts as his comrades joined him singly. Such concerts invariably produced rations.

Federal cavalry officers, especially Philip Sheridan, used bands to inspire headlong charges of his men. Among the Confederate troopers, however, only the famed 2nd Virginia regiment had a band, which came into being by the capture of the instruments of a New York infantry regiment at Haymarket, Virginia.

The 17th Virginia Infantry had Irish music from its fife-and-drum team, composed of a father and his son, the latter so small that his coattails dragged the ground behind, and his drum bumped in front.

A German, Jacob Gans, was the favorite bugler of the Confederate General, Nathan B. Forrest; he was so often under fire as to qualify as a combatant. On one march to Pulaski, Mississippi, riding close to his commander, Gans got three bullet holes in his bugle.

Another German, Jacob Tannenbaum, who had been a court musician in Hanover at nineteen, was caught in Mississippi at the outbreak of war. In Mobile, Alabama, he teamed with Harry McCarthy to write "The Bonnie Blue Flag," according to one story, but soon migrated to the North and joined a minstrel troupe.

One Major Noquet, an engineer on the staff of the Confederate General, Braxton Bragg, endeared himself to troops by his singing in camp, especially a spirited rendition of the "Marseillaise"—but on the eve of the battle of Missionary Ridge he absconded with $150,000 from the army's money chest, deserted to the enemy and told all he knew of Bragg's position.

Late in the war Confederate troops were still being cheered by bands, despite all handicaps. When General Jubal A. Early moved into the outskirts of Washington in 1864, one of the first reports of danger came from a scout, to this effect:

"The enemy are preparing to make a grand assault on Fort Stevens tonight. They are tearing down fences and are moving to the right, their bands playing. Can't you hurry up the Fifth Corps?"

The bands of the 11th and 26th North Carolina (the latter regiment almost destroyed in the engagement) played so loudly during the second day's fighting at Gettysburg as to draw fire from Federal artillery. These men were called from their duty of nursing the wounded to bolster the morale of the infantry, and played for hours in competition with the massed fire of guns on both sides.

One of the war's lively musical traditions was created by J.E.B. Stuart, the cavalry chief of the Army of Northern Vir-

ginia. He fashioned a sort of primitive jazz band around a servant, "Mulatto Bob," who played the bones; Sam Sweeney of
Appomattox, Virginia, a banjoist; half a dozen fiddlers, singers
and dancers. Stuart kept some of them busy through most of the
war; battle was a temporary interruption.

Sweeney was one of the early blackface minstrels. His
brother, Joe, who died just before the war, was credited with
development of the banjo from a crude instrument used by
Negroes on Southern plantations. The Sweeney company had
become so famous as to stage a European tour, and once played
for Queen Victoria.

Stuart was an enthusiastic serenader, and at 1 A.M. of October 9, 1862, just as he was taking his horsemen on one of his
famed raids into Pennsylvania, he paused for a musical interlude.

With banjo, bones, fiddlers and chorus, Stuart roused the
bevy of young ladies at The Bower, the home of Stephen Dand-
ridge, near Martinsburg, Virginia. While his audience smiled
down, the commander of cavalry directed this program—all
within sound of his troops:

Grand Overture	Orchestra
Cottage by the Sea	Sweeney
Lilly Dear	Sweeney
When the Swallows Homeward Fly	Stuart
Looka Dar Now	Capt. Tiernan Brien
Going Down to Town	Sweeney
Ever of Thee	Sweeney
Money Musk	Orchestra
The Separation	Stuart
I Ain't Got No Time To Tarry	
(Sic! sic! sic!)	Sweeney
Evelyn	Stuart
Lively Piece	Orchestra
Soldier's Dream	Stuart
Old Grey Mare	Sweeney

Of the many songs originated in the war, at least one became a well-known hymn—"Hold the Fort, For I Am Coming."
It was born in an incident of the fighting around Kennesaw

Mountain, Georgia, when the Confederates isolated General J.M. Corse with his 1,500 men in Allatoona.

When a division of 6,500 Southerners attacked the outpost, and all seemed lost for the bluecoats, signalmen flapping their flags on Kennesaw Mountain sent Corse the messages:

Sherman is moving with force. Hold out.

And:

Hold on. General Sherman says he is working hard for you.

Corse did hold out, despite 705 casualties and 200 lost as prisoners. Near the end, when Sherman sent a message asking if Corse had been wounded, the defiant reply went back:

I am short a cheekbone and one ear, but am able to whip all hell yet.

Of these materials Philip Paul Bliss wrote his popular hymn.

Perhaps the best-known of all Civil War music is the bugle call, "Taps," which began life as a call for troops of the Federal General Daniel Butterfield.

Music was often a peacemaker of sorts. In the fighting before the fall of Atlanta, the brass band of Major Arthur Shoaff's battalion of Georgia Sharpshooters gave to the cause their expert cornettist. Each evening after supper, the musician came to the front lines and played for Confederates along the entrenchments. When firing was heavy, he failed to appear.

Across the lines, Federal pickets would shout, "Hey, Johnny! We want that cornet player."

"He would play, but he's afraid you'll spoil his horn."

"We'll hold fire."

"All right, Yanks."

The cornettist would then mount the works and play solos from operas, and sing tunes like "Come Where My Love Lies Dreaming," and "I Dreamt I Dwelt in Marble Halls" in a fine tenor.

Colonel James Cooper Nisbet, who was on hand, never forgot the scene: "How the Yanks would applaud! They had a good cornet player who would alternate with our man."

The concert over, firing would be resumed.

8

War in the Air

ONE of the more bizarre scenes of the war unfolded for a stunned audience at Washington's Columbian Armory on June 18, 1861.

A giant balloon, the *Enterprise*, inflated with 20,000 cubic feet of gas and gay with British and American flags, swayed over the capital's treetops.

She carried a full set of signal apparatus. Beneath her trailed an invisible innovation, a hairlike wire wrapped in green silk, which was paid out from a reel at a station below.

The master of the globe was no less spectacular than his vehicle. He was Dr. Thaddeus Sobieski Constantine Lowe (his name was erroneously reported in the Official Records), son of a New Hampshire politician and husband of a French beauty, the daughter of an officer of Louis Philippe's Royal Guard. Dr. Lowe had excited much of the country for several years with his threats to sail on a transatlantic voyage using the eastward-moving currents of air high over the ocean.

The balloon rose 500 feet in the June sky. There was soon the historic chattering of a telegraph key at the ground station.

The message was addressed to President Lincoln:

> Sir: This point of observation commands an area nearly 50 miles in diameter. The city, with its girdle of encampments, presents a superb scene. I have pleasure in sending you this first dispatch ever telegraphed from an aerial station. . . .
>
> T.S.C. Lowe

Other messages were sent from the balloon to distant cities by regular wire. Lincoln replied to his telegram and when the demonstration was over, a crew towed the balloon through the city's streets and anchored it on the White House lawn. Lincoln inspected it from an upper window. The *Enterprise* spent the night there, and the next day Lincoln took a closer look. Some reporters said that he actually made an ascension with Lowe.

All this was a prelude to the first formal use of aerial observation by armed forces, but though Lowe was to become the first chief of the Federal Balloon Corps, he had predecessors as an aerial warrior.

The first balloon bought for American military use was an $850 model of raw India silk built by one John Wise of Lancaster, Pennsylvania.

The officer who sponsored Wise was Major Hartman Bache, the grandson of Benjamin Franklin, who had been the first American to suggest the use of balloons in war. Wise and his gas bag reached Washington before the battle of Manassas, but they missed the fighting despite heroic efforts.

A crew towed the balloon from Washington with a mule-drawn wagon, dodging trees and telegraph poles for hours on a dark night—then struggling down a canal bank, the crewmen often flung into the water in an effort to guide their monstrous charge. An officer who heard the guns of Bull Run in the distance impetuously whipped up his mules and, abandoning rope controls, tore the balloon in trees and deprived the Federal Army of its expected observation post.

The repaired balloon escaped from Washington a few days later and was saved from Confederate hands only by alert troops who shot down the southbound runaway. Wise resigned amid sharp criticism, having served without pay, rations or lodging.

The first really effective balloon observation on behalf of an army came on July 31 at Fortress Monroe, Virginia, with the canny General Ben Butler as sponsor. The balloonist was John LaMountain of Troy, New York, an aerialist who had gained prewar fame by sailing 1,100 miles in less than twenty hours in an eastward trip from St. Louis.

LaMountain found that Confederate camps surrounding the fort were less menacing than Butler had imagined. He also provoked the first known report on military aviation when the Confederate Colonel Robert Johnson sent the message: "The enemy made two attempts to inspect us in balloons."

It was also LaMountain who used the first "aircraft carrier," when he hitched his balloon to the armed transport *Fanny* and rose above the waters of the Chesapeake to peer at the enemy, August 1, 1861. This aeronaut added more firsts by making a night aerial reconnaissance, this time anchored to a tug near Fortress Monroe. He estimated Confederate strength within his view by counting the number of tent lights. He provoked the first "blackouts," for General Beauregard had his camp lights covered and dimmed where the balloons operated.

It remained for Professor Lowe to outstrip all rivals and organize the army's balloon corps. He also designed the first "true aircraft carrier," the converted coal barge USS *George Washington Parke Custis,* which he fitted for efficient balloon ascensions.

Both Lowe and LaMountain, who were hired as civilians, were paid about ten dollars a day plus expenses, but the professor, though much younger and less experienced, became the dominant figure in the war's aerial operations. He established several "firsts" in his career.

He was fired upon by the pioneer "antiaircraft" battery in August, 1861, near Arlington. His opponent, Captain E.P. Alexander, CSA, who was to become a military balloonist himself on occasion, reported that his guns threw shells so near the Federal balloon that Lowe "came down as fast as gravity could bring him."

The birth of modern artillery fire control by aerial reconnaissance was in September, 1861, near Washington's Chain Bridge; later in the war Lowe's men directed Federal mortar fire with great accuracy.

The balloon chief drew from the press ridicule which has

a strange sound in modern ears. The most cutting, by a Cincinnati newspaper, was a satirical report that "an army of airborne troops" would leave "Camp Whatawhopper" to relieve a Federal fort in Florida. But alert officers saw the great value of Lowe's work, and General McClellan went aloft with him several times.

Despite the intense interest of public and some military men, the corps was disbanded in June, 1863, after service on both Eastern and Western fronts. At its peak it had no more than seven trained balloonists in the field, and half a dozen balloons. Some possibilities were overlooked—aerial photography, for example, which was proposed, but not used.

Only one corpsman is known to have died in action, a civilian telegraph operator from Washington, D.D. Lathrop, who stepped on a Confederate "booby trap" torpedo at the base of a telegraph pole near Yorktown, Virginia. The blast tore off his legs and killed him.

The balloons were usually made of pongee in double thicknesses, each sewn by a team of fifty seamstresses, and fashioned in gored sections. A valve at the top of the bag was sealed with a gum of paraffin, beeswax, and other substances, to be opened by a rope when the operator wished to descend. Excess gases could escape from an open tube at the bottom of the sac. The gas was hydrogen, produced in mobile equipment from the action of sulphuric acid on iron filings. Wagons carried wooden tanks which were lined for the purpose, and gases were cooled in copper pipes passed through water and purified by passage through lime.

Only once, during the retreat of the Seven Days battles before Richmond, did Confederates capture aerial equipment, but they then nabbed three gas generators, ready for action.

The Confederate balloon service was skimpy indeed, and there are few recorded instances of its work. The first ascension is said to have been made by Lieutenant John Randolph Bryan on the peninsula below Richmond, a flight cut short by the close firing of the enemy, which soon drove Bryan to earth— where he tried to resign from ballooning. General Joseph E.

Johnston declined sharply: "Absolutely not! You're the only experienced balloonist in the Confederate army."

On another occasion, General Beauregard is said to have sent up a balloon he obtained from "private sources," but the ascent was not successful. The Creole general was undismayed; he later used a balloon in the defense of Charleston.

Lieutenant Bryan got his fill of the balloon service on a final flight when his bag escaped and he drifted over Federal lines. In panic, he destroyed his identification papers and the notes he had made. When the wind changed and he floated over water, Bryan dropped his clothing overboard, prepared to swim for his life.

He landed at last on land, in the midst of a Confederate camp where he was unknown. He was for a time in danger of being shot as a spy, and persuaded the soldiers that he was one of them only after a desperate harangue.

Federals once thwarted Rebel ingenuity. General Longstreet recorded that some unsung hero proposed that the South be called upon for an ultimate sacrifice—the silk dresses of its women. They came in, evidently in plenty, for the general wrote:

> We soon had a great patchwork ship of many varied hues which was ready for use in the Seven Days campaign.

The only source of gas was Richmond, and the balloon was inflated there, tied to a locomotive, and run down the York River Railroad as far as possible. One day, when it was on a steamer going down the James River toward battle, disaster struck. The tide went out, and boat and balloon were left helpless on a sand bar. Longstreet mourned it:

> The Federals gathered it in, and with it the last silk dress in the Confederacy. This capture was the meanest trick of the war and one that I have never forgiven.

9

The Machine Gun

THE deadly stutter of the machine gun rang over several Civil War battlefields, thanks to the vision and persistence of Abraham Lincoln, but its value as an exterminator was lost on the nation, thanks to a stubborn Federal chief of ordnance.

In early June, 1861, Lincoln met the first known salesman of machine guns, J.D. Mills of New York, who led the President to the loft of a carriage shop near Willard's Hotel. Lincoln was an immediate convert.

The gun was mounted on artillery wheels, and atop its barrel was a hopperful of empty metal cartridge cases which dropped one by one into a revolving cylinder as Lincoln turned a crank. Each cartridge was struck by a firing pin and ejected.

"A coffee-mill gun," Lincoln said. The name stuck for the duration of the war, though Mills insisted upon calling it "The Union Repeating Gun." Not even the name of its inventor is now known, though it was probably the conception of Edward Nugent or William Palmer, New Yorkers who battled over its patent rights.

A few days after Lincoln's inspection, the gun was fired at the Washington arsenal before the President, five generals, and three Cabinet members. Some of the generals wanted the gun at once, and Lincoln pressed his chief of ordnance, General James W. Ripley, for action. For months he got none.

Ripley was in his middle sixties, an overworked veteran of almost half a century in the army. He presided over a tiny ordnance office of sixty-four men. He had always been hardheaded; as a lieutenant in the war against the Creeks he had defied Andrew Jackson in behalf of army regulations, and had been threatened with hanging if he did not obey orders. He had served at Fort Moultrie in Charleston Harbor during the first Secession crisis, also under Andy Jackson.

Ripley believed that the Civil War would be short, and that orthodox weapons were essential. He protested against the flood of new weapon proposals on the ground that the army still lacked conventional small arms. He was secretive to the point of denying personal information to editors of an encyclopedia. After three years of war in which he struggled valiantly to arm the Union forces in his own way, he was forced to retire, derided by the press as an old fogy. He had managed to block many a promising new weapon.

Lincoln was also stubborn. He saw two or three other rapid-firing guns in 1861, and in October, when Salesman Mills returned with ten of his coffee-mill guns, Lincoln bought them without consulting anyone, at a price of $1,300 each. It was the first machine-gun order in history.

Not long after, on December 19, 1861, General McClellan bought fifty of these guns on a cost-plus basis; they eventually cost $735 each.

Two weeks later a pair of the guns went into the field for their debut. The officer involved was Colonel John Geary, a seasoned hero of the Mexican War, first Mayor of San Francisco, Governor of Kansas, later to become Governor of Pennsylvania. He presided over the first battle test of machine-gun fire—without knowing whether it was in the least effective.

His 28th Pennsylvania Volunteers guarded some twenty-four miles of the Potomac around Harpers Ferry, and it is surmised that in one of the frequent skirmishes here in January-February, 1862, some Confederate soldier became the first victim of the "rain of death."

On March 29, in a later test with the enemy at Middleburg, Virginia, there was still no one to make an accurate estimate of the worth of the guns. But of Middleburg, at least, there is a suggestion of proof. A Captain Bartlett, in a discussion a month later at New York's Cooper Institute, said that a coffee-mill gun opened fire on Confederate cavalry at 800 yards, cutting it to

pieces, and forcing survivors to flee. The Confederates, in any event, did not know what hit them, perhaps because the guns used conventional Minié balls.

Whatever the mysterious captain thought, Colonel Geary was unimpressed, for on April 28 he returned the guns to Washington, saying that after many trials he must reject them as "inefficient and unsafe to the operators."

There were other trials. General John C. Frémont, the colorful explorer who commanded in West Virginia, sent insistent dispatches to Ripley, saying that experiments with the coffee-mill guns were "satisfactory" and demanding that he be sent sixteen of them. Ripley replied characteristically:

> Have no Union Repeating Guns on hand, and am not aware that any have been ordered.

When the President was called into the controversy, Ripley countered with the unfavorable report filed by Geary—and Frémont was soon gone from his doorstep, defeated by Stonewall Jackson, shuffled in command, and resigned from service.

There dangled from this record a mystery, however: When Jackson captured Frémont's stores at Harpers Ferry, a Richmond newspaper listed as among the loot "17 revolving guns."

In April, 1862, from near Yorktown, a New York *Post* reporter wrote the first account of a machine gun in action. He accurately described the hopper and crank, said that half a dozen of the weapons were used by the 56th New York Volunteers, Colonel Charles H. Van Wyck commanding, and added, "The balls flew thick and fast, and the Yankee invention must have astonished the other side."

There were occasional mentions of the guns thereafter as McClellan advanced on Richmond. Several Pennsylvania regiments were armed with them. It was June 28, at Golding's Farm, that George Wills, Company D, 49th Pennsylvania, emerged as the first-known machine gunner, for he got a thigh wound while firing and was embedded in a regimental history.

A few weeks later the *Scientific American* said a requiem for the weapons. They had "proved to be of no practical value to the Army of the Potomac, and are now laid up in a store-house in Washington."

Even afterward officers ordered them from Ripley, who actually sent some to General Rosecrans in the West, though they were delayed in transit and missed the battle of Chickamauga.

Young Captain David Porter of the Federal Navy, stationed on the Mississippi, ordered four of these guns after a test; at forty yards he hit the head of a keg six out of ten times.

And from the Yazoo River front there was the tale of another test of the coffee-mill guns—when a sliver of lead flew from one of the bullets and struck General W.T. Sherman in the leg, the first reported high-brass casualty of the weapon.

Then, belatedly, came a gifted inventor, Dr. Richard J. Gatling, a one-time North Carolina farmboy, who patented a six-barrel machine gun November 4, 1862, and later adapted it to use the new steel-jacketed cartridge. Gatling tried to interest Lincoln, who by then had turned to other weapons, and few of the improved guns got into service. General Ben Butler ordered a dozen, and one of these is said to have helped kill Confederates near Petersburg as the end of the war drew nigh. Three of the weapons helped guard the New York *Times* building in the draft riots of July, 1863.

The guns were to make Gatling rich and famous, even to the point of commemoration in gangster parlance: "gat." But the doctor bore the taint of being a Copperhead, reputedly a member of the secret society plotting to seize border states for the Confederacy, and his reputation worked against his gun, especially since he was said to have offered it to the Confederates, as well.

It was more than a year after the end of the war, August 24, 1866, when the United States Army became the world's first to adopt a machine gun—Gatling's.

10

A General's Grammar

A BODY of literature has grown from the unlikely question: "Did General Nathan Bedford Forrest, CSA, really say that the rule of success in war was 'Git thar fustest with the mostest'?"

The question persists despite repeated denials and affirmations, and cannot be finally solved.

Numerous letters in the hand of Forrest leave little doubt as to the spirit of informality in which the general came to grips with the King's English. No less obvious is the vigor of his mind, one bit of evidence to support the claim that he was the most gifted and daring field commander in the war.

General Forrest was evidently given as brief training in letters as in formal military tactics.

A sample letter, written from Corinth, Mississippi, May 23, 1862, to D.C. Trader of Memphis:

> Sir Your note of the 21 is to hand I did not fully understand the contents and ask for information—this amount you ask for—is it a publick contrabution or is it my dues due the log [lodge] I wish you would give me the amt due the log from me as you did not state it in your notice or the amount asked for.
>
> I had a small brush with the enemy on yesterday I succeeded in gaining their rear and got in their entrenchments 8 miles from hamburg and 5 behind farmington and burned a portion of their camp at that place they was not looking for me and I taken them by surprise they run like Suns of Biches I captured the Rev. Dr Warren from Illa-

noise and one fine sorel stud this army is at this time in
front of our entrinchments I look for a fite soon and a big
one when it comes off cant you come up and take a hand
this fite will do to hand down to your childrens children
I feel confidant of our success.

Yours respect
NB Forrest

11

How Young They Were!

IT might have been called The Boys' War.

Authorities differ, and statistics bristle in the controversy, but this is the offering of the *Photographic History of the Civil War:*

More than 2,000,000 Federal soldiers were twenty-one or under (of a total of some 2,700,000).

More than 1,000,000 were eighteen or under.

About 800,000 were seventeen or under.

About 200,000 were sixteen or under.

About 100,000 were fifteen or under.

Three hundred were thirteen or under—most of these fifers or drummers, but regularly enrolled, and sometimes fighters.

Twenty-five were ten or under.

A study of a million Federal enlistments turned up only 16,000 as old as forty-four, and only 46,000 of twenty-five or more.

Yet by other authorities, the Union armies were made up like this: 30 per cent of men under twenty-one; 30 per cent from twenty-one to twenty-four; 30 per cent from twenty-five to thirty; 10 per cent over thirty.

Confederate figures are skimpier, but one sample of 11,000 men produced about 8,000, the great majority, between eighteen and twenty-nine. There was one of thirteen, and three were fourteen; 31 were fifteen; 200 were sixteen; 366 were seventeen; and about a thousand were eighteen. Almost 1,800 were in their thirties, about 400 in their forties, and 86 in their fifties. One man was seventy, and another, seventy-three.

Most of the youths of tender age slipped in as musicians, for there were places for 40,000 in the Union armies alone. There are numerous tales of buglers too small to climb into saddles unaided, who rode into pistol-and-saber battles with their regiments. Most famous of these on the Union side was Johnny Clem, who became drummer to the 22nd Michigan at eleven, and was soon a mounted orderly on the staff of General George H. Thomas, with the "rank" of lance sergeant.

The Generals

Some leading commanders were elderly when war came, notably the Federal Commander-in-Chief, Winfield Scott, who was seventy-five. General John Wool was seventy-four, Edwin V. Sumner was sixty-four, and John Dix sixty-three.

The dean of ranking Confederates was the Adjutant General, Samuel Cooper, who was sixty-three. Albert Sidney Johnston was fifty-eight. Robert E. Lee and Joseph E. Johnston were fifty-four.

Most of the war's famous general officers in the field were young. A partial list of these, and their ages at the outbreak of war in 1861:

Seventeen: Brevet Major General Galusha Pennypacker, USA, the youngest of the war's general officers. Born June 1, 1844, and too young to vote until the war's end.

Twenty: Brigadier General William P. Roberts, a North Carolina cavalryman, who was the youngest Confederate general.

Twenty-one: George A. Custer, USA, born in December, 1839, and a cavalry brigadier in June, 1863, at age twenty-three.

Twenty-three: Judson Kilpatrick, USA, West Point, '61, a brigadier and major general in 1865, at the age of twenty-seven.

Twenty-four: W.H.F. (Rooney) Lee, son of Robert E. Lee, and Stephen D. Ramseur, CSA.

Twenty-five: The cavalrymen, Joe Wheeler, CSA, and Wesley Merritt, USA, the former a major general at twenty-six, the latter a brigadier two days before Gettysburg, at age twenty-seven.

Twenty-six: Godfrey Weitzel, USA, the corps commander who ruled fallen Richmond; Fitz Lee, CSA; and Adalbert Ames, USA, West Point, '61.

Twenty-seven: William Dorsey Pender, CSA.

Twenty-eight: The cavalrymen, Alfred Torbert, USA, and J.E.B. Stuart, CSA, and Stephen D. Lee, CSA.

Twenty-nine: John B. Gordon and Custis Lee, CSA.

Thirty: Philip Sheridan, USA, and John B. Hood, CSA.

Thirty-one: O.O. Howard and Gouverneur K. Warren, USA.

Thirty-two: Carl Schurz, USA.

Thirty-three: George Crook and J.B. McPherson, USA, and Patrick Cleburne and George A. Pickett, CSA.

Thirty-four: Lew Wallace, USA.

Thirty-five: George B. McClellan, USA, and John H. Morgan, CSA.

Thirty-six: A.P. Hill and William Mahone, CSA.

Thirty-seven: Stonewall Jackson and E. Kirby Smith, CSA, and Ambrose Burnside, USA.

Thirty-nine: U.S. Grant, USA.

Forty: James Longstreet, D.H. Hill, Nathan B. Forrest, and John C. Breckinridge, CSA.

Forty-one: William T. Sherman, USA, and Earl Van Dorn, CSA.

Forty-three: P.G.T. Beauregard, CSA.

Forty-four: Richard S. Ewell and Braxton Bragg, CSA.

Forty-five: Jubal A. Early, CSA.

Forty-six: George G. Meade, USA.

Forty-seven: Joseph Hooker, USA, and John C. Pemberton, CSA.

Many other youthful figures came to fame in the war:

John Wilkes Booth was twenty-six when he murdered Lincoln.

John Pelham, the famed Confederate cannoneer, entered the war at twenty-three, and two years later was dead, just before he was promoted from major.

Bennett A. Young, a Kentucky cavalryman who was trained under John Hunt Morgan, led the sensational Confederate raid on St. Albans, Vermont, in October, 1864, at the age of twenty-one. With his band of twenty-six he "captured" the town, robbed its banks of some $200,000, and fell back to his base in Canada, almost fatally disrupting Anglo-American relations as a result.

Arthur MacArthur of Wisconsin, who failed to get into crowded West Point in 1861, wangled a place as adjutant of the 24th Wisconsin at the age of seventeen, and a year later was a colonel. He commanded a regiment at the bloody battles of Resaca and Franklin, and was thrice wounded. He went into the regular army, and retired in 1909 as the last lieutenant general of his era. He was the father of General Douglas MacArthur.

Nelson A. Miles made a reputation as a fighting young officer early in the war, and was kidnaped from his company of the 22nd Massachusetts by men of the 61st New York and made their colonel. In May, 1864, when he was twenty-six, he became a general, and served thirty-eight more years in the Army, retiring as lieutenant general.

No one knows the identity of the war's youngest soldier, but on the Confederate side, in particular, there was a rush of claimants. Some of their tales belong with the war's epic literature:

George S. Lamkin of Winona, Mississippi, joined Stanford's Mississippi Battery when he was eleven, and before his twelfth birthday was severely wounded at Shiloh.

T.D. Claiborne, who left Virginia Military Institute at thirteen, in 1861, reportedly became captain of the 18th Virginia that year, and was killed in 1864, at seventeen. (This likely belongs with the war's apochrypha.)

E.G. Baxter, of Clark County, Kentucky, is recorded as enlisting in Company A, 7th Kentucky Cavalry in June, 1862, when he was not quite thirteen (birth date: September 10, 1849), and a year later was a second lieutenant.

John Bailey Tyler, of D Troop, 1st Maryland Cavalry, born

in Frederick, Maryland, in 1849, was twelve when war came. He fought with his regiment until the end, without a wound.

T.G. Bean, of Pickensville, Alabama, was probably the war's most youthful recruiter. He organized two companies at the University of Alabama in 1861, when he was thirteen, though he did not get into service until two years later, when he served as adjutant of the cadet corps taken into the Confederate armies.

M.W. Jewett, of Ivanhoe, Virginia, is said to have been a private in the 59th Virginia at thirteen, serving at Charleston, South Carolina, in Florida, and at the siege of Petersburg.

W.D. Peak, of Oliver Springs, Tennessee, was fourteen when he joined Company A, 26th Tennessee, and Matthew J. McDonald, of Company I, 1st Georgia Cavalry, began service at the same age.

John T. Mason of Fairfax County, Virginia, went through the first battle of Manassas as a "marker" for the files of the 17th Virginia at age fourteen, was soon trained as a midshipman in the tiny Confederate Navy, and was aboard the famed cruiser *Shenandoah*.

One of Francis Scott Key's grandsons, Billings Steele, who lived near Annapolis, Maryland, crossed the Potomac to join the rangers of Colonel John S. Mosby, at the age of sixteen.

War closed many schools and colleges, and sent thousands into war, North and South. Washington College of Virginia sent a little company of sixty-four in the first days of war, their average age about seventeen, their average weight about 130 pounds. Of a total of sixty-five present in the two battles of Manassas, twenty-three were killed or wounded—and in the forty battles in which it fought with the 4th Virginia Infantry, the company lost 100 dead or wounded, and forty-six captured, of a total strength of 150 from recruitments.

In South Carolina, it was a Citadel cadet who fired the first shot of the war, against the steamer *Star of the West* as she sought to relieve the Fort Sumter garrison.

The University of Virginia had 530 men enrolled from the Southern states: 515 of them joined the Confederate service.

The 1st Arkansas Infantry included students of St. John's

College of Little Rock, their ages reported from fourteen to eighteen in 1861.

The most celebrated schoolboy performance of the war was the baptism of fire of the Virginia Military Institute Cadet Corps at the Battle of New Market, Virginia—the only such instance in the war. The action took place in the Shenandoah Valley outside the village of New Market, in rolling country between a fork of the Shenandoah River and the flank of Massanutten Mountain. It was fought May 15, 1864, between a Federal force of some 6,500 under General Franz Sigel and Confederates about 4,500 strong, under General John C. Breckinridge.

The Cadets had marched in from Lexington, leaving the younger ones on their campus disconsolate, feeling disgraced at missing the opportunity to fight. The corps was 215 strong when it reached New Market, and was put into the opening battle on Sunday morning. They were eighteen or under, some of them sixteen, and reputedly even younger. (Tradition has it that some were only fourteen.)

They marched behind their commander, Lieutenant Colonel Scott Shipp, twenty-four, who rode a dappled gray horse. The boy soldiers heard their first cheering near the front, as General Breckinridge rode by "like the Cid," in the words of young John Wise, son of a Virginia governor.

Boys in an artillery battery recognized friends among the cadets as they passed, and called gibes:

"Here come the wagon dogs! . . . Ho, bombproofs, get outa them good clothes."

Some cadets wanted to fight for their honor on the spot, but were herded on. John Wise and three others were left behind as a baggage guard, but he made a dramatic speech to his crew and they deserted the post, leaving a Negro driver in charge of the wagon; they joined the cadet column.

Henry Wise, another of Governor Wise's sons, was one of their captains; the night before he had chided the boy soldiers for cursing, and for chicken stealing, but had later eaten some cold fowl in camp with them.

About noon, when a black thundercloud hung over the val-

ley, the cadets joined the Confederate line of battle in the center
—the place of honor, the history-conscious among them thought.
They came to a hill crest, passed their own little battery in
action, and went down a slope into the open.

They heard musket fire and artillery, but nothing seemed
close until a clap burst overhead. Five men went down in C
Company: Captain Govan Hill, and Merritt, Read, Woodlief,
and John Wise. Just before he lost consciousness Wise saw
Sergeant Cabell look at him with a pitying expression.

"Close up, men," Cabell said.

The line reached a ravine within 300 yards of a busy Federal
battery—the six fine guns of the 30th New York, under Captain
Albert von Kleiser. The ravine gave cover from the cannon,
which fired from a crest studded with young cedars. The ditch
was filled with cedar scrub, briers, stones, and stumps, and the
cadets were a few minutes in passing through; even so, they were
out before the older veterans on their flank, the 62nd Virginia.

Once the cadets halted under heavy fire while the file
straightened, and the advanced flanks came even with the center.
A dwelling, the Bushong House, split their line, and by companies they passed on either side, marking time beyond, restoring
the line once more.

Colonel Shipp halted them. "Fix bayonets," he said. Almost
immediately he was struck by a shell fragment, and fell. Several
cadets were wounded at this moment, and the file lay down.
Someone yelled an order to fall back on the next Confederate
unit, but Cadet Pizzini of B Company swore and said he would
shoot the first man who moved backward.

Captain Henry Wise got to his feet and shouted for a charge
on the guns, and the line went up after him.

A Federal Signal Corps captain, Franklin E. Town, on the
hill beside Von Kleiser's battery, watched the cadets come on
with such fascination that it did not occur to him that he might
be captured. The big guns had already changed from shrapnel
to canister and then double canister, so that the air was filled
with murderous small iron balls. The cadet corps did not falter,
and in these last yards lost most of its dead and wounded.

Captain Town saw: "They came on steadily up the slope.

. . . Their line was as perfectly preserved as if on dress parade.
. . . Our gunners loaded at the last without stopping to sponge,
and I think it would have been impossible to eject from six guns
more missiles than these boys faced in their wild charge up that
hill."

The cadets were soon among the Federal gunners with bayonets. Lieutenant Hanna felled one with his dress sword, and
Winder Garrett caught one with his bayonet. One cadet found
Lieutenant Colonel W.S. Lincoln of the 34th Massachusetts on
the ground, pinned by his fallen horse, but still defiant, and ready
to shoot with a cocked pistol; the cadet subdued him with a
bayonet.

With wild yells the cadets greeted the sight of the Institute
flag over the guns, waved by their tall ensign, Evans, and celebrated their victory on the hilltop while the rainstorm broke.

Of John Wise's disobedient baggage guard of four, one was
dead and two were wounded. The corps had eight dead and
forty-four wounded, all told.

The 62nd Virginia, charging beside them, had seven of its
ten captains shot down, four dead, and a total of 241 killed and
wounded.

The chase went on for three miles as Sigel's force withdrew
to Rude's Hill and beyond, and there was fighting, especially by
artillery, after dark.

The next day, when he passed the VMI battery at the roadside, General Breckinridge stopped to pass compliments:

"Boys, the work you did yesterday will make you famous."

Dave Pierce, a boy soldier not too young to understand
military life, called back: "Fame's all right, General, but for
God's sake where's your commissary wagon?"

An impressive ceremony still a part of VMI life today
celebrates May 15 on the Lexington campus. Selected cadets at
roll call snap their replies as the names of the New Market
casualties are called: "Dead on the field of honor, sir."

12

Famous Onlookers

THE landscape of war was crowded with figures marked for later fame, most of them cast in minor roles in the conflict itself.

In the dusk of an April Sunday in 1862, Confederate infantrymen stormed the last center of Federal resistance on the first day of the battle of Shiloh. Among them were troops from Arkansas.

In the ranks of the 6th Arkansas was a twenty-year-old private who went by the name Henry M. Stanley. He had come up from Cypress Bend with the Dixie Greys—and would one day lead an African expedition ending in the famous greeting: "Dr. Livingstone, I presume?"

Captured at Shiloh, "Stanley," whose real name was John Rowlands, enlisted in the Union Army, was shortly dismissed because of poor health, and joined the Union Navy—only to desert at Portsmouth, New Hampshire, in 1866.

The Abolitionist stronghold of Lawrence, Kansas, suffered burning and massacre on a terrible August day in 1863. One hundred and fifty men were left dead by Confederate guerrillas. The leader of the band was W.C. Quantrill, and with him rode men who were at the beginnings of careers which would terrorize the West and embed them in folklore. With the raiders were the infamous Younger Boys. One of their companions was the youthful Jesse James.

Abraham Lincoln's funeral procession, rolling down New York's Broadway on April 25, 1865, was watched by two small boys from a second-floor window at Fourteenth Street. They were Theodore Roosevelt, age six and a half, and his younger brother Elliott, the future father of Eleanor Roosevelt. The boys were nephews of the Confederate chief of secret service in Europe, James D. Bulloch.

When a Confederate force under General Jubal A. Early reached Washington's gates on July 11, 1864, Lincoln narrowly missed death at the hands of a sniper. As a man fell dead beside the President, a young officer tugged at Lincoln, who was on a parapet. "Get down, you damn fool, or you'll be killed."

Lincoln clambered down to safety and smiled at his savior: "Well, Captain, I see you have already learned how to address a civilian."

The captain was Oliver Wendell Holmes, Jr., the Magnificent Yankee of the future.

As one of history's first observation balloons hung over the battlefields before Richmond in 1862 a foreign observer studied the gas-filled floating bag with interest. He was Count von Zeppelin, a Prussian observer, father of the dirigible.

A fortyish little red-haired society woman from Boston, wife of Dr. Samuel Gridley Howe, visited Washington early in the war. When she crossed the Potomac to visit an army camp Mrs. Howe heard a passing regiment chant a familiar air, "John Brown's Body," and a companion asked her casually, "Why don't you write more suitable words to that song?"

Mrs. Howe was aroused in her Willard's Hotel room that night by another marching column singing the John Brown song, and as she drowsed new words came into her mind. She forced herself to rise and scribble them on some sheets of stationery, the lines flowing with hardly a pause. She rewrote few words in the stanzas which were to become a veritable theme song of the war: "Mine eyes have seen the glory . . ."

Next morning she was astonished to find the completed poem, having forgotten its writing. She recovered, however, and sold it to the *Atlantic Monthly* for four dollars.

In a sharp little fight at Lexington, Kentucky, in December, 1862, General Nathan Bedford Forrest took the town for the Confederacy, drove out some Illinois cavalry and nabbed their colonel, a Peoria intellectual who was to become celebrated as the leading American agnostic, Robert G. Ingersoll. The young heretic was discovered in a hiding place under the porch of a house, and was ousted by his captors with much difficulty.

Jefferson Davis, a captive on his way to a Federal prison, rode with Vice-President Stephens in a carriage through Augusta, Georgia, in the strange spring of 1865. An eight-year-old boy peered at them through blinds of the Presbyterian minister's house, absorbing a scene he would not forget. He was Woodrow Wilson.

A darkened blockade-runner slipped from the Cape Fear River on the North Carolina coast near the end of 1863, bound for England. She bore as a passenger a war-weary woman, Mrs. Anna McNeill Whistler, who was off on a visit to her son, a painter. She got a warm welcome in London, part of which endures in the painting famous today as "Whistler's Mother."

Though he did not set foot on American soil, a German writer excited readers North and South with his five hundred-odd dispatches to Horace Greeley's New York *Tribune*, which appeared until the coming of war. The author was a radical social scientist already banished from his country, the father of an obscure thirteen-year-old document, *The Communist Manifesto*, Karl Marx. Historians suspect that, though he financed his work on *Das Kapital* by sale of his articles to Greeley at five dollars each, they were actually written by his friend and benefactor, Friedrich Engels.

In March, 1862, as the battle for Western territory neared a climax, the Federal General, Samuel R. Curtis, sent ten scouts into Rebel lines, all disguised as Confederates. The party passed freely among the Southerners, who were moving in strength toward a battle position to be known as Pea Ridge and/or Elk-

horn Tavern. The captain of this troop of scouts soon came in with his report. He was James Butler Hickok, a long-haired young man with formidable mustaches, who was to become widely known as Wild Bill.

A seventeen-year-old musician of Company K, 42nd North Carolina Regiment, went through illness, prison guard duty, the battles at Petersburg and Cold Harbor, and the fall of Fort Fisher before his capture in March, 1865. He emerged from prison in June by taking a loyalty oath to the Union, and began the long walk home to the Carolina hills.

The enemy could not spell Tom Dula's name, and persisted in rendering it "Dooley," so that Tom signed his loyalty oath both ways, in compromise. He began his trek southward with new hope, unaware that tragedy lay ahead for him—a nightmare trial for murder of his sweetheart, followed by execution. He was the incipient hero of the folk ballad which was to sweep the country almost one hundred years after him: "Hang down your head, Tom Dooley. . . ."

When the Confederate cruiser *Alabama* went down off Cherbourg, in battle with the USS *Kearsarge*, hundreds of Frenchmen watched from shore; they had been invited to the conflict, which was announced in advance by the Confederate skipper, Admiral Raphael Semmes.

One of the French audience was Edouard Manet, then at the threshold of a distinguished career as a painter. He was so impressed that he painted the battle scene, now a treasure of a Philadelphia art gallery.

In the flame-lit streets of Richmond on April 3, 1865, as the Yankee invaders burst in, the ten-year-old son of the departed chief of Confederate ordnance, General Josiah Gorgas, took over as man of the family. Young Willie struggled to help his mother carry furniture from the apartment in the government armory.

The family left the building in a colorful procession, Willie dragging the terrified cow, followed by his mother with four young daughters clinging to her skirts and an infant boy in her arms. The armory's shells began exploding and a fragment struck the cow, which bolted, knocking Willie to the ground.

In the safety of his Aunt Maria's Richmond house Willie found no rest, for he was posted all night on the rooftop, where he beat with wet rags at cinders which fell on the shingles.

Willie grew up to be Dr. William C. Gorgas, a public-health hero as conqueror of yellow fever and the man who made possible the Panama Canal.

In a battle near Lynchburg, Virginia, in June, 1864, a former Vice-President of the United States, Confederate General John C. Breckinridge, faced two future Presidents in uniform—General Rutherford B. Hayes and Major William McKinley. (Four other Union generals went to the White House: Grant, Chester A. Arthur, James A. Garfield, Benjamin Harrison.)

A big, handsome spinster of thirty entered a converted hotel in Georgetown known as Union Hospital in December, 1862. She was a volunteer nurse come down from Concord, Massachusetts, to aid the wounded.

A sheltered woman who had seen little of death and suffering, she spent her first morning in watching a soldier die and comforting a boy with a bullet through his lungs. She had hardly begun when wounded from the battle of Fredericksburg overran the hospital.

The new nurse went to the old hotel ballroom to greet them: "The first thing I met was a regiment of the vilest odors that ever assailed the human nose." She carried a vial of lavender water to combat these as she worked with the men of torn and shattered bodies; surgeons amputated without anesthetics, but the young nurse's most fearsome duty was that of scrubbing the survivors with cakes of dark brown soap.

Within a few weeks she became ill—typhoid pneumonia was the diagnosis—and was taken home, expected to die. She lived to become known as creator first of *Hospital Sketches* and then of *Little Women*, Louisa M. Alcott.

The blockade-runner *Lucy*, escaping to sea from Wilmington, North Carolina, in a storm of November, 1864, carried as signal officer a young army veteran who kept a flute up his sleeve, and in leisure moments tootled romantic airs. The captain was British, and there was a supply of British uniforms aboard for use as disguises in case of capture.

In the Gulf Stream just fourteen hours out of port, the *Lucy* was caught by the USS *Santiago de Cuba*. The captain gave his signal officer the ship's purse for distribution among the crew, and the youngster was so generous as to give most of his share to an old seaman who had been overlooked. The signaler declined to pull on a British coat and save himself, and went overboard to a Federal prison pen at Point Lookout, Maryland.

He lived through four terrible months in prison, and it was probably there that he contracted tuberculosis of which he later died. He celebrated the prison in his first book; he was Sidney Lanier, who became in his brief life the most celebrated Southern poet of his time.

As Abraham Lincoln was inaugurated on a raw March day of 1861, the scene was recorded by a twenty-five-year-old youth who perched far out in the throng, sketching away with a pencil. He was a magazine illustrator whose rendition of the historic moment would soon appear as a two-page drawing in *Harper's Weekly*, and whose sketches of the war would lead him to water-color and oil painting and make him one of the country's great native artists, Winslow Homer.

Amid the first day's bloody fighting at Shiloh, when Federal remnants huddled under a bluff of the Tennessee River, a sergeant of the 9th Indiana came upon a steamer which bore reinforcements. He met a small woman on deck who brandished an ivory-handled pistol, shouting that she would do her duty like a man, if worst came to worst. The sergeant would not forget: "I'm proud to remember that I took off my hat to this little fool."

The sergeant was soon busy aiding in the effort to beat back frightened soldiers who tried to board the steamer for safety. The sergeant was Ambrose Bierce, the strange writer in whose vivid fiction the war was to live long after the guns fell silent.

13

Which War?

THE conflict known to most of us as the Civil War has a long and checkered nomenclature. Some samples:

The War for Constitutional Liberty
The War for Southern Independence
The Second American Revolution
The War for States' Rights
Mr. Lincoln's War
The Southern Rebellion
The War for Southern Rights
The War of the Southern Planters
The War of the Rebellion
The Second War for Independence
The War to Suppress Yankee Arrogance
The Brothers' War
The War of Secession
The Great Rebellion
The War for Nationality
The War for Southern Nationality
The War Against Slavery
The Civil War Between the States
The War of the Sixties
The War Against Northern Aggression
The Yankee Invasion
The War for Separation
The War for Abolition
The War for the Union

The Confederate War
The War of the Southrons
The War for Southern Freedom
The War of the North and South
The Lost Cause

To this day some patriotic Southerners wince at the term, Civil War. These partisans usually favor The War Between the States—and some organizations of descendants of Confederate warriors use this term under their by-laws, and none other. The title seems to stem from the two-volume work by Alexander Stephens, the Confederate Vice-President, published after the war.

Most of the names listed are of Southern origin, since the defeated and their heirs grasped for some expression of unquenched ardor and defiance which would do justice to the Old South. These names have been seriously, not to say apoplectically, offered to the world.

In more jocular vein the war has been known as The Late Unpleasantness, The Late Friction, The Late Ruction, The Schism, or The Uncivil War. But in the South in particular it is known simply as The War, as if the planet had not heard a shot fired in anger since '65.

There is confusion of a similar sort as to the very names of Civil War battles. Familiar to students of the conflict, these are baffling to newcomers.

The root of the difficulty was geography; invading Union armies lived by maps, while Confederates were at home with the terrain and, in addition, usually chose the field of battle. As a result, Federals often named battles for nearby streams, while Confederates used the names of towns. For example:

Federal	Confederate
Bull Run	Manassas
Antietam (Creek)	Sharpsburg
Stone's River	Murfreesboro
Fair Oaks	Seven Pines
Elkhorn Tavern	Pea Ridge

Union armies were also named for streams, as The Army of the Potomac, The Army of the James, The Army of the Tennessee. Confederate counterparts were The Army of Northern Virginia, The Army of Tennessee, and the Trans-Mississippi.

14

John Brown Ignites a War

FEW incidents have so accurately forecast the future as the John Brown raid on Harpers Ferry in October, 1859.

Brown invaded the town as the armed vanguard of Abolitionism, more daring than his backers in the North. He could not stir the slaves to rebellion, but his handful of whites and Negroes drew to the spot a surprising number of the chief actors of the war drama soon to open. Historic omens marked the end of old Brown.

At the time of the raid Brown's notoriety rested chiefly on the Pottawatomie Massacre of May, 1857, when he had killed five proslavery men in the bloody frontier war. It happened that twenty-five years earlier, almost to the day, young Captain Abraham Lincoln visited that Kansas village—where he watched some of his troops of the Black Hawk War mutiny and desert.

One of Brown's first captives at Harpers Ferry was a living symbol of the Republic, Lewis Washington, a great-grand-nephew of the first President. Brown took from him a sword given to George Washington by Frederick the Great; he used it throughout the raid. When Brown's party was besieged in a fire-engine house and those outside hesitated to attack for fear of wounding the hostages, it was Washington who shouted for them to fire.

One who heard him was the Army colonel in command, Robert E. Lee, who said, "The old Revolutionary blood will tell," and sent in his shock troops—Marines.

The man who led his charging detail was James Ewell Brown Stuart, a lieutenant who, like Lee, happened to be on leave from his Western cavalry post. The Marines took Brown's force in three minutes, suffering but one casualty, and the Marine commander, Lieutenant Israel Green, sabred Brown into submission.

The Marines had been sent by Secretary of War John Floyd, who was soon to become a Confederate general; they had been reinforced with Virginia troops sent by Governor Henry A. Wise, also to become a general in gray.

In the watching crowd as Brown was grilled after his capture, all gathered in a tiny room:

Congressman A.R. Boteler of Virginia, who became Stonewall Jackson's liaison with Richmond; Senator J.M. Mason, of Mason-Slidell fame; Governor Wise, Major Lee, Lieutenant Stuart, and Congressman Clement L. Vallandigham of Ohio, who would emerge as leader of a vast wartime Copperhead conspiracy against the Union.

Brown went to prison to await trial and execution, and more Virginia troops came to the area, among them the Richmond Howitzers. With the artillerymen came one of the most popular novelists of the day, John Esten Cooke, a brother-in-law and future aide of Jeb Stuart.

The Virginians were besieged with pleas of mercy for John Brown, including one from his family, which offered insanity as the cause of his crimes: Nine relatives on his mother's side, six of his first cousins, and two of his children were insane. His wife died insane. An alienist was ordered to examine Brown, but no tests were made.

When Brown was hanged in Charles Town, Virginia, his passing was witnessed by others marked for fame:

Professor Thomas J. Jackson of the Virginia Military Institute commanded state troops; within less than two years he would become famous as Stonewall Jackson. He prayed for Brown as the old man fell through the scaffold at the end of his rope.

In the ranks of the Richmond militia was a boy actor, John Wilkes Booth.

Pressing near the ranks of soldiers was old Edmund Ruffin, the agricultural expert and prophet of Secession.

As Brown dangled from the gibbet a young Virginia artist and illustrator violated his last privacy by lifting his blindfold to sketch the grim face. The resulting story and pictures were rejected as inflammatory by *Harper's Weekly*, but the young artist-reporter became widely known as Porte Crayon, prolific in drawing and writing of war scenes—and under his real name, D.H. Strother, as a Federal general.

On the day Brown was hanged, December 7, 1859, Henry Wadsworth Longfellow sat at his desk in distant Massachusetts and wrote prophetic lines:

This will be a great day in our history; the date of a New Revolution—quite as much needed as the old one. Even now as I write they are leading old John Brown to execution in Virginia for attempting to rescue slaves! This is sowing the wind to reap the whirlwind which will come soon.

15

The Widow Fritchie

A QUAINT small house in Frederick, Maryland, a lure to thousands of tourists in season, is a 1927 restoration of a shrine to an enduring heroine of the Civil War famed for an act of patriotic defiance she almost certainly did not commit.

In the first week of September, 1862, when Lee's army first invaded the North, Mrs. Barbara Hauer Fritchie, widow of a Frederick glovemaker, was almost ninety-six years old, and bedridden.

A niece who lived across the street recalled that the old lady was abed throughout the Confederate occupation of the village, and did not so much as glimpse Stonewall Jackson, let alone scold him into legend. She could not have seen Jackson as he entered Frederick, since he came in an ambulance, the victim of a fractious horse. The weight of testimony says she did not see him as he left.

Dr. Lewis H. Steiner of the United States Sanitary Commission had the presence to sketch the vivid events of the week. He was dismayed by the sight of Jackson's troops:

> A dirtier, filthier, more unsavory set of human beings never strolled through a town—marching it could not be called. . . . Faces looked as if they had not been acquainted with water for weeks; hair, shaggy and unkempt. . . . Many of them were without shoes. . . . The odor of clothes worn for months, saturated with perspiration and dirt, is intense and all-pervading.

Their only decent music, the doctor said, was made by a Negro bugler. But Steiner was not misled by appearances. These men were "stout and sturdy, able to endure fatigue and anxious to fight. . . . They all believe in themselves as well as their generals, and are terribly in earnest."

There were few incidents to catch the doctor's eye, but one casual paragraph in his report to Washington bore the seed of a folk tale:

> A clergyman tells me that he saw an aged crone come out of her house as certain rebels passed by trailing the American flag in the dust. She shook her long, skinny hands at the traitors and screamed at the top of her voice, "My curses be upon you and your officers for degrading your country's flag." Her expression and gestures as described to me were worthy of Meg Meriles.

This could hardly have been Barbara, or Jackson. Stonewall's troops marched by the Fritchie house, to be sure, but by a well-documented account, the general himself left his men at West Second Street to pay a visit to friends at the Presbyterian parsonage, and rejoined them by a short cut, emerging well beyond Barbara's door.

When the Rebels had gone, Old Barbara came out of her house, her niece said, where she leaned feebly on her cane, waving to incoming Federal troops from her porch. Her niece brought out a tiny American flag which was kept in the family Bible—a small silk banner with thirty-four stars, on a staff less than a yard long. Barbara waved this to the troops. A few officers stopped to wring her hand and bless her.

Within a few days, when the armies were fighting at Sharpsburg, west of Frederick, the tale of Barbara's defiance of Jackson was already current. Mrs. Fritchie's role was merged with that of the anonymous woman in Dr. Steiner's pages—though another elderly woman of the town laid futile claim to the honor.

The story was passed by Barbara's niece to C.S. Ramsburg of Georgetown, who had it published in a Washington newspaper, and told it to his neighbor, Mrs. E.D.E.N. Southworth, then America's leading romantic novelist. This lady immediately thought of John Greenleaf Whittier. The Quaker poet was moved by her tale of the incident, and wrote in response the thirty couplets which so resounded with the bootfalls of the Rebel army and rang with patriotic fervor as to lift Barbara, Frederick, and General Jackson to glory.

Whittier sent the poem to his editor, James R. Field of the *Atlantic Monthly*, and got this reply:

> Barbara is most welcome and I will find room for it in the October number, most certainly. . . . You were right in thinking that I should like it, for so I do, as I like few things in this world. . . . Enclosed is a check for fifty dollars, but Barbara's weight should be in gold.

A few days later Whittier wrote Mrs. Southworth:

> I heartily thank thee for thy kind letter. . . . It ought to have fallen into better hands, but I have just written out a little ballad of Barbara Frietchie which will appear in the next *Atlantic*. If it is good for anything thee deserves all the credit for it.

Mrs. Southworth's narrative had been almost unchanged by Whittier as he compressed it into verse, the chief improvement in the ringing words of Barbara as she faced Rebel fire. Mrs. Southworth had reported her as crying unpoetically, "Fire at this old head, then, boys; it is not more venerable than your flag."

The ballad was an immediate hit, reprinted in wholesale fashion, and quickly on its way to immortality with generations of American school children:

> Up from the meadows rich with corn,
> Clear in the cool September morn, . . .
>
> "Shoot, if you must, this old gray head,
> But spare your country's flag," she said. . . .
>
> "Who touches a hair of yon gray head,
> Dies like a dog! March on," he said. . . .

A shrewd Confederate in the Richmond *Examiner* soon hailed the poem as a masterwork:

Verse is stronger than prose and history is powerless in competition with the popular ballad. . . . The unculti- vated may pronounce the poem so much unadulterated and self-evident nonsense, but the wise . . . know it will out- live and disprove all histories however well authenticated.

Battle raged over the authenticity of the ballad for years. Witnesses continued to bob up, including some Confederate soldiers who testified to its truth. Whittier clung to his story, and in 1888 replied to a critic:

The poem was written in good faith. The story was no invention of mine. It came to me from sources which I regarded as entirely reliable; it had been published in news- papers, and had gained public credence. . . . I had no rea- son to doubt its accuracy then, and I am still constrained to believe that it had foundation in fact. . . . I have no pride of authorship to interfere with my allegiance to truth.

Even the spelling of Barbara's name bred controversy. Whit- tier favored *Frietchie,* as did many afterward. The spelling used here follows contemporary sources in Frederick, including Bar- bara's family and Dr. Steiner.

Of all this Barbara knew nothing. She died two weeks be- yond her ninety-six birthday in December, 1862, months before she appeared in the lines of the ballad. An obituary in a Frederick newspaper gave brief mention to her passing—but of her clash with Stonewall Jackson and her immortal defense of the Stars and Stripes, not a word.

16

Imported Warriors

The Union

ONE historian says, only half in jest, that two Swedes won the Civil War: Admiral John Dahlgren, who revolutionized naval power in prewar years by developing big guns for United States warships; and John Ericsson, who created the fantastic *Monitor*.

Dahlgren's big guns in small wooden ships, a scheme Europeans thought impossible, doomed the tiny Confederate Navy and made the blockade effective, at least against foreign intervention.

Ericsson's *Monitor*, which sneaked into Hampton Roads in the nick of time to prevent the Confederate *Virginia* from breaking the blockade, was an equally bold innovation. (Earlier Federal ironclads on the Mississippi were of much simpler design.)

These were but two of the tens of thousands of foreign-born who helped the United States win the war. Six major generals were born abroad, probably including Sheridan, whose birthplace is in doubt—and even George Meade was born in Spain, though of American parents. In this group is Julius Stahel, who is given major credit for making Federal cavalry effective; he won the Congressional Medal of Honor at the Battle of Piedmont, and in the Hungarian Revolution won the Cross of Bravery.

Among brigadier generals were nine Germans, four Irishmen, two Frenchmen, a Russian, a Hungarian, a Pole and a Spaniard.

In 1860, the North had three fourths of the foreign-born.

John
Ericsson

The census of that year shows almost 4,000,000 foreigners in the North, and 233,000 in the South. Half of these had arrived in the preceding ten years—and were one reason for the defiance of Southern leaders, who saw the balance of population and power slipping from them.

Germans took the lead as war opened, and made up ten regiments in New York, six in Ohio, six in Missouri, five in Pennsylvania, four in Wisconsin, three in Illinois—with scatterings everywhere. One of a dozen half-German Illinois regiments was the 82nd, which had an all-Jewish company, the wealthiest outfit in the army, sponsored by business leaders in Chicago. From its ranks Edward Salomon rose to command, and it became known as a valorous company.

The 31,000 Germans in Missouri who went into blue saved the Western frontier for the Union; four fifths of the St. Louis Union men were foreign-born, chiefly German.

The Irish were not far behind; the Harp of Erin flew on their green flags over every major battlefield. Two Massachusetts regiments were pure Irish, as were three others in New England, four in New York, two each in Pennsylvania and Indiana.

Thomas F.
Meagher

Brigades and regiments came from Ohio and Illinois. New York's Irish Brigade, one of the most famous, was virtually wiped out at the battle of Fredericksburg—much of the blood spilled by a corresponding brigade of Confederate Irishmen.

New York sent out a French regiment, with Spaniards, Germans, Italians, and one company of native Americans on its rolls; the latter was poorest, and lacked discipline. These men were the renowned Gardes Lafayettes; by July, 1862, only 400 survived.

New York also had a Scotch regiment, infused with Irishmen; its men drank heavily, and led a mutiny after the first battle of Bull Run/Manassas, refusing to go back into Virginia from a Washington camp. Their colors were taken and some were jailed; the regiment later fought bravely.

Scandinavians filled many companies, and there were Swiss, Welsh, Dutch, and Mexican outfits. One Mexican regiment in New Mexico was routed by Confederates in its first encounter.

The GARIBALDI GUARDS

The 39th New York, the Garibaldi Guard, was unique. Experts say that not even the free lances of the Middle Ages produced its like.

Its Colonel was George Utassy, a Hungarian; its lieutenant colonel was Italian; its surgeon, German. Ranks were filled with English deserters, Swiss, Croats, Bavarians, Cossacks, Garibaldians, Sepoys, Germans, and Algerian Zouaves of the French Foreign Legion. There were three companies of Hungarian Hussars, three of German infantry, one of Italian Carabineers, one of Swiss, one of French *Chasseurs à Pied*, one of Spaniards and Portuguese. Most were veterans of European wars.

They mutinied once and retreated into Washington, but were controlled, and gave good service throughout the war. The 39th flew the Hungarian flag of red, white and green stripes, and its regimental colors were some which Garibaldi had planted in Rome. This regiment had few survivors in '65.

Garibaldi himself was offered a commission, for he was much sought as liberator of the divided Italian states. The agents of Secretary of War Seward combed the world for officers. General George Klapka, a hero of the 1849 Hungarian Revolution, when approached, laid down remarkable terms: $100,000 in advance, a salary of $25,000 a year, a post as chief of the general staff until he learned English—after which he would replace George McClellan as General In Chief.

Another famous New York regiment was the 69th, the Zouaves of General Thomas Meagher, an Irishman who was condemned to death in a native rebellion, was instead banished to Tasmania, and escaped to America in 1852. He had many brilliant, though less well-known, contemporaries.

The Russian, General John B. Turchin, captured Huntsville, Alabama, in 1862, led heroic charges at Chickamauga and Missionary Ridge, and commanded a cavalry division in the Army of the Cumberland.

Count Luigi Palma deCesnola, a veteran of the Italian and Crimean wars, was a brave brigadier who led a charge against Jeb Stuart's horsemen at Aldie, though unarmed and under arrest at the time. General Judson Kilpatrick gave him his sword to finish the action. The Italian was wounded and captured in the next charge, but after a term in Libby Prison was exchanged and later fought in the Shenandoah campaign.

A Swedish brigadier, Charles A. Stohlbrand, was a favorite of Sherman's, and after his capture at Atlanta and an escape from Andersonville Prison, he was pushed to high rank by old "War Is Hell," who took the case to Lincoln.

There were numerous titled soldiers and adventurers, and among the leading knights errant were the Bourbon princes from France, the Comte de Paris and the Duc de Chartres, caught in the country at the outbreak of war, and volunteers who served the Union armies without pay. No mere observers, they rode as General McClellan's aides, often on dangerous night duty.

Baron von Vegesach, a Swede, appeared on many Virginia battlefields, and at the head of the 20th New York led a wild charge on the Confederate center at Antietam/Sharpsburg. In that battle, when told that his high-flying flag was drawing fire on his Germans, the Baron refused to lower it. "It is our glory!"

(Many foreign-born died on this field: When the Irish Brigade went through The Corn Field to relieve General Hooker's men it lost half of one regiment and 30 per cent of another; its green flag went down five times. And it was the 79th New York, the Scots, who fought their way into the village of Sharpsburg just before the Confederate A.P. Hill arrived to save the day for the South.)

There was Prince Felix Salm-Salm, a monocled Prussian cavalry officer of thirty, who spoke no English and served as General Blenker's chief of staff. When he was taken to see President Lincoln, and someone revealed he was a prince, Lincoln slapped him on the back: "That won't hurt you with us."

Sir Percy Wyndham, of a noble British family, had fought for France, England, Austria, and Italy, and had been knighted by Victor Emmanuel. He was badly wounded at Brandy Station and returned to Italian service.

Among the mystery men of the war was one "Major Warrington," a middle-aged man of red face and graying hair, and a haughty, cultivated manner. Army gossips whispered that he was an illegitimate son of George IV. He disappeared at the battle of Fair Oaks/Seven Pines while carrying a message under fire.

There were the Swedish Barons, Jacob von Cedarstrom and Ludwig von Holstein, and the German, Baron Otto von Steuben, killed at Spotsylvania. There was also the Austrian, Count Gustavus Saint Alb. All told, 57 titled German officers are known to have served in the Federal armies.

Among the lower ranks was Captain Peter Kiolbassa, a Confederate who was captured, enlisted as a Federal private, and rose to captain once more, this time with the 6th U.S. Cavalry.

One of the foreigners at Gettysburg was Sergeant Frederick Fuger, a German with Battery A, 4th New York Artillery, left in command during Pickett's Charge when all his officers were hit. He fought his one remaining gun with such bravery as to win a gold medal.

One of the casualties of Gettysburg was an eighteen-year-old English boy who fell with a Massachusetts regiment—the son of the explorer, David Livingstone. He probably died in prison at Salisbury, North Carolina.

Foreigners on both sides deserted. One of the more colorful cases was that of one Black, a Scot who had Southern relatives, and joined the Union army in hopes of crossing the lines. On guard duty on the Potomac River one day, while pretending to take a bath, he struck out for the Virginia shore, yelling, "Goodbye, boys. I'm bound for Dixie." He escaped under fire.

One night while Black was guarding a group of captured Federals, a captain recognized his voice—the new Confederate was escorting his old company. Black explained, "I hope you and the boys are all right, Captain. It's not because I didn't want to fight that I left you. I like to fight in the right cause."

The Union Navy, too, had strong cadres of foreign-born. Admiral Farragut's flagship, *Hartford*, had twenty-five nationalities aboard at one time; almost two thirds of this ship's crew (216 of 324) were born outside the United States. Irish and British made up most of the crew.

Several other large United States ships had crews of from a half to two-thirds foreign-born. And the USS *Kearsarge*, in her famed victory over the Confederate *Alabama*, had a crew of which a quarter were foreign-born.

The Confederacy

Though many foreigners, especially the freedom-loving Germans, shunned the slave-owning South (and called the Confederate flag *Klapperschlangenflagge*—Rattlesnake Flag) Dixie attracted thousands of outlanders to her service. Of the Confederate Cabinet, Secretaries Judah Benjamin, C.G. Memminger, and Stephen Mallory had been born abroad.

Five Southern generals were born in Ireland, more than many native states produced. Three more came from France, and two from England. Of the Confederate major generals, two of the most colorful were the Irishman Patrick Cleburne, "The Stonewall Jackson of the West," a British Army veteran; and Camille Armand Jules Marie de Polignac, a prince of French royal blood, a Crimean War veteran who was sent to woo Napoleon III for the Confederacy. Polignac, put in command of some wild Texas cow hands who had been dismounted for service, was threatened with mutiny. The men swore that "no frog-eating Frenchman we can't pronounce will command us." They transformed his name into "Polecat" and held their noses when he approached. When he understood this, young Polignac broke the resistance of his men by marching them over rough terrain in search of polecats; the Texans grew to love the hard-fighting Frenchman.

Among Southern brigadiers:

Xavier B. Debray, France; John A. Wagener and Robert Bechem, Germany; Peter Alexander Selkirk McGlashan, Scotland (this man rose from private, and his was the last commission signed by Jefferson Davis in his flight); Collett Leventhorpe, and William M. Browne, England; Patrick T. Moore, Walter P. Lane, James P. Hagan, and Joseph Finnegan, Ireland.

A sampling of the legion from abroad serving as colonels and lieutenant colonels:

Marquis de Marcheville and P.F. deGournay, France, the latter a New Orleans newspaper editor who raised and equipped an artillery company; Santos Benavides, Mexico; Count Arthur Grabowski, Hypolite Oladowski, Valery Sulakowski, Frank Schaller, and Ignatius Szymanski, Poland; Bela Estvan, Austria; Heros von Borcke, Germany; August Forsberg, Sweden; George Gordon, England; Adolphus H. Adler, Hungary (this man, on the staff of General Henry A. Wise, criticized his superior as "No soljare," was suspected of treason, thrown into Libby Prison, and escaped to the North).

Heros
von Borcke

One of the striking captains in service was the Englishman, John Cassons, the "wild man" of General Law's staff who was captured after a wound at Gettysburg, escaped from Johnson's

Island, and stole his way South—only to find on a farm near Richmond a widow of such charm that he claimed exemption as a foreigner, married and settled down.

Justus Scheibert, the Prussian captain, was an observer who saw much of the Gettysburg action from the top of a tree on a knoll—a post so good that General R.E. Lee came twice to the foot of the tree to question him.

A popular post for foreign adventurers was aide-de-camp, and few Southern generals were without these companions; three foreigners became chiefs of staff (von Borcke to Jeb Stuart; St. Leger Grenfell to John Morgan; and Victor von Scheliha to Simon Bolivar Buckner).

Among the best-known aides:

Marcus Baum, a German Jew who served General Joseph B. Kershaw and made a reputation for gallantry and loyalty; the Prussian Barons, von Massow and Barke.

Another German Baron, William Henry von Eberstein, enlisted with the Washington Grays of the 7th North Carolina and was named Fifth Sergeant.

Bennett G. Burleigh, an Englishman, ran the blockade from New York to Richmond, carrying a model of a submarine battery invented by his father, but was clapped into prison by suspicious Confederates and held until he got the ear of the naval expert, Captain John Brooke.

Many thousands of foreigners are known to have been in Confederate ranks, but accurate figures are lacking. One Canadian of the time claimed that 40,000 of his countrymen fought for the South, almost surely an exaggeration.

The 1st Louisiana was probably the champion mixed regiment, for it sported men of thirty-seven nationalities. The Deep South furnished so many men of French nativity and descent that the Confederate army had two "official languages." In testimony to this fusion, General Beauregard invented the expression, "sacredamn."

Louisiana furnished three Zouave regiments, many of the men recruited from the New Orleans slums. Recruiting booths were opened in prisons, and criminals were offered their choice of the army or life in a cell. The resulting collection of troops caused strife wherever it appeared; Zouave privates once stole a train en route to Montgomery, Alabama, after unhooking the officers' car. They stole, fought, and wrecked villages and towns; at least one regiment was disbanded.

The Avegno Zouaves, recruited from a higher stratum of society, also had a reputation for wildness; in their ranks were Frenchmen, Chinese, Mexicans, Italians, Spaniards, and Irishmen.

A third Louisiana Zouave regiment which became famous bore the name "Tigers," and was commanded by the Crimean War veteran, Rob Wheat; a couple of these men were shot for insubordination, and at least once the Tigers killed civilians in a melee.

There were companies of Germans, Frenchmen, Poles, Italians, Spaniards, and Mexicans. A European Brigade and several Irish regiments were in service. One company of Italian laborers was formed. Richmond had a Foreign Legion, made up mostly of Englishmen. Wilmington, North Carolina, furnished Company A of the 18th North Carolina, of which all but 30 of 102 were German-born. Charleston turned out many German units, including cavalry—but especially artillery. The Irish Volunteers of the first company to volunteer "for the war" came from Charleston.

Georgia sent out eight companies of foreigners, most of them Irish and German. Tennessee had an Irish regiment under Pat Cleburne, and Texas sent Germans, Mexicans and Poles. Louisiana's Foreign Legion included a company of Belgians and one of Swiss. The European Brigade of the same state had 2,500 Frenchmen, 800 Spaniards, 500 Italians, 400 Germans, Dutch and Scandinavians, and 500 Swiss, Belgians, English and "Slavonians."

Among the "galvanized Yankees"—made up of captured Federals wearing Confederate gray—were two battalions formed in 1864 at the suggestion of a German, Conrad Nutzel. These

converts enlisted for three years. Irishmen were preferred, but
Germans were allowed; the South took a good many who claimed
to be British, and one of these units staged a mutiny at the siege
of Savannah and its leaders were executed.

One of Nutzel's galvanized companies, made up of Germans,
behaved gallantly at Egypt Station, Tennessee, against Grierson's
raiders and fought under hopeless conditions for several hours
before becoming prisoners of war. Many captured Confederates,
on the other hand, fought in blue as "Galvanized Rebs."

Though the Southern foreign-born population was relatively
small, Richmond's immigrants, mostly German, equaled 23 per
cent of the native white population in 1860. In Charleston the
percentage was higher. Almost a quarter of the people of Mobile
and New Orleans were foreign-born when war came. Texas had
421,000 whites, three fourths of them recent immigrants to the
state, and a tenth of them foreign-born. This was the only state
whose aliens dared oppose the Confederacy, and many Texas
Germans fled to the north. Since a fifth of the Texans were
German, even Negroes spoke the language, and there were
German newspapers, schools and churches.

In Company I, 8th Alabama, 104 of the 109 men were Irish-
born, and the men wore dark green uniforms; their banner was
a Confederate battle flag on one side with a full-length figure of
George Washington in the center. The reverse was green, with
a harp, shamrocks, and the slogans, "Erin-go-bragh" and "Faugh-
a-ballagh."

The Louisiana Polish Brigade of two regiments, formed by
Major G. Tochman, a veteran of the Polish Revolution, was a
violent mixture which included Irishmen, Germans and Americans, most of them deck hands from the Mississippi and Gulf
trade. Several of these men were killed when they staged a riot
at Grand Junction, Tennessee.

Foreigners aided the Confederacy in many fields:
M.J.R. Thomassy, a French geologist, produced salt by solar

evaporation, and developed salt wells in Alabama and mines in Louisiana.

The blockade-runner, *R.E. Lee*, ran aground coming into Wilmington, North Carolina, in 1862, but managed to put ashore much good lithographing equipment and twenty-six Scottish lithographers—all useful in printing money and stamps. The firm of Ludwig & Hoyer in Richmond, the most famous in its field of lithography, had foreign workmen, chiefly German.

A Swiss, Henry Hotze, was taken from the 3rd Alabama and sent to London as a propagandist for the Confederacy. He founded an influential paper, *The Index*, fed Southern news and opinion to British and Continental newspapers, and plastered London with colored posters of the Confederate and British flags intertwined.

Hotze gained a virtual monopoly of American news in Europe by wooing the official French news agency, and once stirred a furor by persuading the influential Presbyterian press in England to circulate to its readers a defense of slavery by Southern clergymen.

Louis Haiman and Brother, a firm of German tinners, had the South's largest sword factory in Columbus, Georgia, a plant covering a city block, its five hundred employees turning out one hundred swords weekly in addition to other items, including revolvers.

The Mexican, Juan Quintero, opened the northern tier of Mexican states to Confederate trade, and made possible smuggling and free passage of arms, men, and supplies of great value to the South.

John William Mallet, a chemistry professor at the University of Alabama, Irish-born, and a Ph.D. from the University of Göttingen, graduated from a lieutenancy in infantry to the ordnance laboratory at Macon, Georgia, where he worked miracles.

Father Abram J. Ryan, an Irishman, wrote the most famous Confederate war poem, *The Conquered Banner*. He lost a brother in the Southern army.

Patrick Lynch, an Irish civilian, saved scores of buildings and homes in the burning of Atlanta, fighting flames with crews of slaves when the Federal Army burst in.

General Patrick Cleburne, the Irishman, attempted a political coup for the South, but was balked by Jefferson Davis, General Joseph E. Johnston, and other leaders until it was too late. Cleburne suggested in 1864 that the South arm all able-bodied slaves and promise them freedom in the event of victory—a course he thought would force the North to withdraw its armies and might bring European recognition. It was also the only way to strengthen Confederate forces.

Captain Charles Murray, an Englishman, later Lord Dunmore, served three years on a blockade-runner and then on Robert E. Lee's staff. He was a descendant of Virginia's last Royal Governor.

Among the dead at Shiloh the South lost Hugh McVey, an Irishman over seventy years old, a veteran of Waterloo who had enlisted in Company D, 4th Kentucky, CSA.

An eleven-year-old bugler in the same battle turned the tide for the Orphan Brigade when its flag fell and an old cannon was lost. "Little Oirish" took the banner to the captured gun, mounted it, and screaming and waving the flag, prompted a charge.

When the cruiser *Alabama* fought the USS *Kearsarge* off the French coast, two Englishmen drowned aboard her were Dr. David Herbert Llewellyn and an assistant engineer, William Robinson. Most cruiser crews were made up largely of Englishmen, and this was the case on the *Alabama*, though there were also Danes, Irishmen, and one Russian (or a Finn—the record is not clear).

"Captain Roberts," skipper of the blockade-runner *Don*, was really the Honorable Augustus Charles Hobart Hampden, son of the Earl of Buckinghamshire, once commander of Queen Victoria's yacht. He made a fortune, and the *Don* was captured on her first voyage after he left her.

The blockade-runner *Condor* was commanded by Admiral Hewitt of the British Navy, who had been knighted by Victoria as Ambassador to Abyssinia. He was the skipper who put the Rebel spy, Rose Greenhow, into a small boat off Wilmington, North Carolina, on the night she drowned.

17

The Rains Brothers

IN the first month of 1864 an expert from the Confederate Torpedo Bureau entered the office of Jefferson Davis with a curious object—an iron casting, heavy and black, for all the world like a lump of coal. The President, turning it in his hands, pronounced it "Perfection itself."

It was a small bomb, designed to be tossed into a Federal coal barge, whence it would be shoveled into an enemy warship's boiler with devastating effect.

The secret weapon was soon in action, and one of its victims was the captured blockade-runner *Greyhound*, which exploded and sank under mysterious circumstances in the James River. The notables, General Ben Butler and Admiral David Porter, were among her startled passengers. Investigators laid the blame to Confederates who had sneaked aboard as "roughly dressed stowaways," planted their bombs in coal bunkers, and fled. Porter sent orders through the fleet that coal barges were to be guarded around the clock—and that strangers found with lumps of imitation coal were to be shot.

This invention was the work of General Gabriel J. Rains, the elder son of a cabinetmaker from New Bern, North Carolina, a West Point graduate who had been mooning over explosives since his days in the Seminole War. His younger brother, George Washington Rains, also a West Pointer, was busy making most of the Confederacy's gunpowder.

The Rains boys were mysterious figures to most of their contemporaries and are largely overlooked by historians, though they were outstanding munitions makers whose innovations did much to improve the art of administering violent death.

Gabriel, fifty-eight when the war opened, was a brigadier general in early '62 when the Federals drove between the York and the James toward Richmond. He made a memorable debut.

Federal cavalry trotted confidently in the sandy roads after the retreating Rebels, but under the hoofs of their horses explosives flared, and casualties were considerable. Many companies bolted in panic. They had stumbled onto the first land mines used in battle, clever little devices made by Gabriel Rains after the earlier design of Samuel Colt, complete even to tin shields against rain.

There were more of these weapons, and the Northern press soon thundered against Rebel barbarity: mines had exploded in wells, around houses, in bags of flour and carpetbags, and around telegraph poles—the counterpart of the modern booby trap had claimed several Union lives. The Confederate commander on the front, James Longstreet, was almost as indignant as the enemy press, and forbade further use of the mines.

Rains denied that he had rigged booby traps, but he took credit for the land mines in roads. The affair became a Confederate policy squabble, for Rains appealed to Richmond over Longstreet's head, and Secretary of War George Randolph (who was Thomas Jefferson's grandson) took the inventor into the War Department where he was safe from Longstreet. Randolph announced the policy: "It is admissible to plant shells in a parapet to repel assault, or in a road to check pursuit. . . . It is not admissible to plant shells merely to destroy life and without other design than that of depriving the enemy of a few men."

Rains reported to President Davis on the possibilities of experimental explosives and was asked to head a Torpedo Bureau; a few months later the bureau filled General R.E. Lee's order for hundreds of torpedoes and mines to bar the James River to enemy shipping. Months afterward Federals were reporting mines in the river, most of them fired by wires leading from the banks. They ranged in size to 1,950 pounds.

At the end of the war the United States Navy reported greater loss of ships from torpedoes than from all other causes

combined. Rains estimated his bag of enemy ships sunk by torpedo at fifty-eight. It was a quiet and still largely unrecognized
revolution in naval warfare.

Rains solved some thorny problems. There was not a foot
of wire in the Confederacy for his electrical mines; he sent
women operatives behind enemy lines to steal. His biggest haul
was an abandoned enemy cable in the Chesapeake Bay, which
he shredded and used in hundreds of mines. The Confederate
Army was also an adversary, both in the struggle for supplies
and claims of victory. For months the Torpedo Bureau squabbled with General D.H. Maury over laurels for sinking the
Federal monitor *Tecumseh* at Mobile.

Rains had too little money for his work. He began with an
appropriation of $20,000 for torpedoes, but though this rose to
$350,000 in 1864—and soon afterward to $6,000,000—it was too
late.

Despite everything, he built torpedo factories at Richmond,
Wilmington, Mobile, Charleston, and Savannah. In one "munitions plant" on the Mississippi a few men under a shed packed
glass demijohns with powder, attached crude ignition devices,
piled them on a wagon, and saw them off under "Old Pat," a
Negro driver whose duty was to drop them into the river, where
the current was to take them among an invading Federal fleet.

By one means or another torpedoes spread through the
Confederacy. Seven of twelve Federal ships on a foray up the
Roanoke River in North Carolina were victims of the floating
mines. Before Fort Fisher, near Wilmington, North Carolina, a
great field of buried torpedoes helped to hold Federals at bay
until the very end of the war. In May, 1864, the USS Steam
Corvette *Commodore Jones*, torpedoed in Virginia waters, was
blown fifty feet into the air, according to witnesses, and lost 147
of her 150-man crew.

Rains said that the Richmond approaches were guarded by
1,300 land mines in 1864, many of them operated by trip cords
to be pulled by hidden Confederates when unwary Union soldiers walked nearby. To prevent Southern deaths in the mine
fields, each torpedo was marked with a red flag by day and a
shielded lantern by night. At the fall of Richmond, Federal

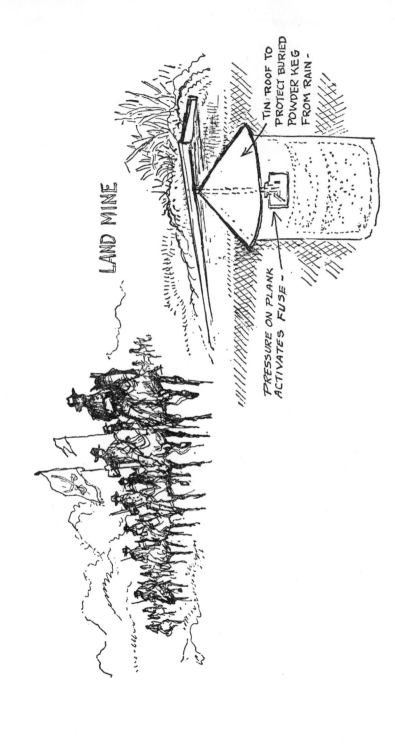

LAND MINE

TIN ROOF TO PROTECT BURIED POWDER KEG FROM RAIN -

PRESSURE ON PLANK ACTIVATES FUSE -

columns were guided through the mine fields by Rebels, but a few incautious bluecoat looters were killed by explosions.

Brother George Rains provided most of the powder for torpedoes, mines, shells, and virtually all other Confederate munitions. George had led the West Point class of '42 in scientific studies and served as professor of chemistry, geology and mineralogy, but when he was assigned to make gunpowder for the Confederate armies had not so much as seen a powder mill.

Rains had operated ironworks in Newburgh, New York, but otherwise had no obvious qualifications as munitions maker. Even so, Chief of Ordnance Josiah Gorgas gave him a free hand.

As Jefferson Davis said, hardly a round of ammunition had been made in the South for fifty years, except during the Mexican War. By the most optimistic estimate there was powder enough for one month of war, providing there was light fighting.

The gunpowder of the day, as George Rains knew well, was made of three-quarters potassium nitrate (known as saltpeter or niter) and small amounts of sulphur and charcoal. It seemed hopeless to find enough of the first two ingredients in the Confederacy, and if they were found, they would be quite impure, making faulty gunpowder inevitable.

Rains went like a prospector into the limestone caves of Tennessee, Alabama, Georgia, and Arkansas, and found earth so rich in nitrate of lime that he put crews to digging it, and later formed a niter and mining bureau. By a simple chemical process—saturation with lye made from wood ashes—he rendered this earth into saltpeter. An idle mill near Nashville, Tennessee, was soon making powder and a stamping mill furnished its ingredients. Rains began on July 10, 1861, and by late October was turning out 3,000 pounds of powder daily at Nashville; since there were no experts, Rains was forced to act as overseer.

He wrote a booklet on collecting saltpeter, gathered a force of newly trained men, and with them at work, returned to Richmond. He sent agents to Europe for more nitrate, and eventually smuggled 2,700,000 pounds through the blockade. Most singular of all, he divided the South into districts, each with crews to dig the earth from privies and latrines, and even collect the contents of chamber pots—all to be dumped into niter beds for processing.

Some of the war's most entertaining bawdy songs came from this practice, on both sides of the lines.

George made progress. By November of '61 he was producing another 1,500 pounds of powder daily in Richmond. He then made an important find—an English pamphlet describing the world's most modern powder plant, the Waltham Abbey Works. Though it contained no drawings, the booklet was so complete that Rains, with the help of C. Shaler Smith, a young architect and engineer, built the finest gunpowder mill of the day. He erected a giant complex which lay for two miles along a canal at Augusta, Georgia, a spot chosen for its safety from Union raiders, and as a central base of supply. The factory was built with materials from every corner of the Confederacy.

The huge Tredegar Iron Works at Richmond built for Rains twelve circular iron plates and twenty-four 5-ton rollers —some 250 tons of machinery. He got four more rollers from Macon, Georgia, and Chattanooga, Tennessee. He ordered from another Tennessee plant an iron shaft almost 300 feet long, a foot thick at the center—an engineering marvel of its time. A gear wheel 16 feet in diameter was fixed to the center of the shaft, giving it motion. This piece of skilled metal work was cast in Atlanta.

Rains found in a cotton mill a steam engine of 130 horsepower with five boilers and a 14-ton flywheel, all made in the North before the war; he took the power system apart and hauled it across the South to its new home. He ordered a dozen iron evaporating pans from works on the Cumberland River, Tennessee, and big retorts and iron slip cylinders from an Augusta shop. Copper boilers were made from converted turpentine and whiskey stills brought in from seaports and backwoods. Tin and zinc for roofing came from Mobile. Iron and coal for castings came from North Carolina and north Alabama and raw copper from Ducktown, Tennessee.

By the end of 1861 the price of powder coming through the blockade had climbed to three dollars per pound—and since Rains made a million pounds that year, he calculated that he

saved the Confederacy almost two million dollars. After spending heavily on his factories, he showed an immense "profit"; his
Augusta plant cost the Confederacy about $385,000.

The maze of buildings concealed many miracles worked by
Rains and his men. Impurities in saltpeter ruined powder by
absorbing moisture, thus it must be crystallized and washed over
and over. The plant consumed from 8,000 to 10,000 pounds
daily; the vital spot was the refinery room.

Rains had cleverly arranged evaporating pans in this room,
with canal water flowing under them for cooling, and hot air
from separate furnaces heating others. The room was thus free
of ashes and smoke. When it was found that the volume was too
great for his working force, Rains devised machinery which
filled the pans, pouring boiling liquid into drains and crystallizing
vats on schedule. One refinement was a vat which agitated during evaporation, so as to produce tiny particles. Soon, Rains
boasted, he could run the process three times daily with only
two or three workmen. His saltpeter he thought "unmatched
anywhere."

A sulphur refinery taxed Rain's ingenuity, for he had to
remove all traces of acid, and his supply was by no means pure.
Most of the sulphur came from Louisiana planters who had imported it before the war to refine their sugar crops. The sulphur
must be treated until, when powdered and evaporated on glass,
it would leave no stain. Distillation was the key Rains used. The
sulphur was melted, poured into wooden boxes 5 feet tall and
10 inches square at the bottom, tapering upwards. As it cooled,
impurities trickled down and the relatively pure upper portion
went into kettles, was vaporized, condensed in water-cooled
coils, then collected in its purity. Rains bolted and pulverized
it like flour before he was done, using iron wheels five feet in
diameter which revolved on a bed of iron. Rains used silk to bolt
his sulphur so long as it lasted, but the South's silk supply was
soon gone. He devised a better scheme.

As the pulverized sulphur was revolved in barrels fastened
on hollow axles, hot air was blown through, depositing the finest
sulphur dust in an adjoining room.

Charcoal was the next problem. Willow was said to make

the best, but this was soon exhausted, and Rains tested cotton-wood, which he found to be equally good. He had the wood split into sticks less than two inches square, and packed them into iron cylinders 6 feet long. Retorts were dropped over the cylinders, covers sealed with clay, and the bottoms perforated to permit the escape of gases—which in turn supplied most of the furnace heat necessary for the process. The wood burned to charcoal within two hours, was lowered into the canal below for cooling, then went into pulverizing barrels, where it was beaten to a powder by tumbling bronze balls. After bolting, it went to the weighing room to be combined with other ingredients. Rains made up charges of 45 pounds of saltpeter, 9 pounds of charcoal and 6 of sulphur.

This mixture was moistened and heated by steam until it became slush; it was then cooled into a cake, a product Rains thought the finest ever processed. He had used his microscope to improve on his British predecessors.

He saw that carbon particles, even when finely ground, were pitted with tiny holes. Since saltpeter was the active ingredient of gunpowder, it should be made to fill these pores. Thus Rains developed the method of reducing the powder to slush, allowing the niter to crystallize partially within the charred carbon. This step also reduced the final rolling process from four hours to one.

Rains had a dozen rolling mills, separated for safety, stretching some 300 feet along the canal. Their walls were ten feet thick in places, with glass fronts in case of explosion. Workmen operated long levers by a friction gear built under the floors, in order to control the dangerous rollers. Above each roller was a thirty-gallon water tank which was connected with each of the other rollers in the mill, rigged to spill its contents at any given moment. In short, any explosion would bring instant drowning of all the cake gunpowder. Rains had but three explosions inside the plant, only one causing injury. But before safety precautions were taken, an accident outside the main plant blew three tons of gunpowder, sending up a 500-foot column of smoke and flame, and killing seven men, a boy and a mule—all the result of a workman smoking in violation of orders.

Bronze wheels, vibrating screens, and sieves finished the powder process, grading the final product. Big guns on the battle fronts, especially the seaports, used powder in pieces an inch square, weighing about an ounce per cube; but small weapons must have the most finely ground powder. Rains also designed a superior powder box to replace kegs for shipment, and reported that there were no explosions in delivery.

He developed an "electro-ballistic" machine to test arms fired with his powder, and duplicated an apparatus for determining the pressure in gun barrels.

Rains produced 2,750,000 pounds of gunpowder at Augusta in three years, furnishing most of that fired by Confederates east of the Mississippi. The plant never worked to capacity, and even when a rush order for 22,000 pounds of powder came from Charleston, it took only two days' production. Powder captured here was used after the war by the United States School of Artillery Practice at Fortress Monroe, and pronounced superior. President Davis said sadly that if such fine powder had been in the magazines of the cruiser *Alabama*, she would have sunk the USS *Kearsarge*, and have been saved for further deadly raids on enemy shipping.

Today, despite the work of these brother geniuses in munitions, readers can find reference to them only by arduous digging. Records of the Confederate Torpedo Bureau are lost and presumed destroyed. The only full account of the Confederate powder factories, written by General George Rains, is one of the rarer Civil War pamphlets, seldom seen except by scholars straying from the beaten path.

18

Riots on the Home Front

CIVILIAN populations were not docile on either side of the Potomac. Criticism of government policies was often bitter, and sometimes led to violence.

The Federal draft act brought on bloody rioting in New York which raged for three days in the nearest approach to revolution during the conflict and left almost 2,000 casualties.

The tragedy opened on July 13, 1863, when a mob wrecked and burned the offices of the Provost Marshal at Forty-third Street and Third Avenue, after destroying the drum from which the names of 1,200 New Yorkers had been drawn for army service.

The blow fell when the state had been stripped of able-bodied men for the battle of Gettysburg. For three days there was no halting the mobs, which had obviously been assembled by plan. Officers suspected John Andrews, a Secession evangelist who gave treasonable harangues on street corners. Also suspected: Governor Horatio Seymour, a strong Democrat who had publicly attacked the draft; former Mayor Fernando Wood, then in Congress, an accused "Copperhead," or Confederate "fellow traveler."

The mob was made up chiefly of Irishmen recruited from slums and inflamed by the cry that they must furnish "poor man's blood for a rich man's war." They protested that they would not go to war while men of means could pay $300 for a substitute under Lincoln's new law.

The crowds surged through much of the city, unchecked even by the entire police force. They burned the draft office on

Broadway and a dozen more buildings. They looted and burned several homes of wealthy families on Lexington Avenue, burned a Methodist church, a Negro orphanage, stores, factories, and saloons where they were refused free liquor.

A young Negro was hanged on Clarkson Street, and men danced and sang around him while a fire roasted his flesh. At least thirty Negroes were shot, hanged or stamped to death, and much of the city's colored population fled. Numbers of policemen were wounded and a few were killed. The mob grew until it was estimated at between 50,000 and 70,000 people. It used guerrilla tactics when police columns or hastily formed Home Guard companies went into action. Many volunteer officers fell under rifle and shotgun fire from windows on upper floors of buildings.

Police Superintendent John Kennedy, who went bravely into the midst of the rioters, was dragged through gutters, thrown into a horsepond, twice savagely beaten, and left for dead.

Police surprised the mob in a swift counterattack, left hundreds lying in the corridors of the besieged New York *Tribune*, and managed to save this and the buildings of the *Times* and *Post,* all objects of the rioters' wrath. The *Times* thought the mobs "the left wing of Lee's army."

Pitched battles continued. Strong parties of soldiers, policemen, and firemen were defeated. A Marine detachment was driven off by a mob on Grand Street. Police barely managed to whisk away a stock of carbines in a government warehouse and, at Thirty-fourth Street and Second Avenue, 300 policemen with two field guns stood off a mob of 10,000, finally clearing the area. Colonel Henry O'Brien of a militia regiment lost his life in an aftermath to this skirmish when a mob caught him on the street, beat and stamped him until he was almost dead, then dragged him to his home, where men, women, and children danced around his body until he succumbed.

Mobs had built barricades on Eighth Avenue between Thirty-seventh and Forty-third, and on First Avenue between Eleventh and Fourteenth. A late night attack by police carried these fortifications, but battles dragged on until troops returned

from Gettysburg, and even then the 7th New York regiment
had to withstand a furious assault by a mob of 5,000 on Second
Avenue. Bricks and gunfire from rooftops killed 15 soldiers
there.

It is possible that these so-called Draft Riots were touched
off by racial prejudice. Not long before, a strike of New York
longshoremen had been broken when Negroes were imported
and placed in their jobs.

As a final touch of irony, police found "The Rebel Spy"
John Andrews in his lair, and arrested him, in company with his
Negro mistress.

Abraham Lincoln stoutly refused to suspend the draft
through all the uprising, despite pleading of New York officials.
He held grimly to his plan to push the war to an end.

Lesser mobs had risen in the South earlier in the year, but
were spurred by hunger rather than anger and prejudice.

In Salisbury, North Carolina, some 75 women, most of
them wives of Confederate soldiers, rose on March 15, 1863,
armed themselves with axes and hatchets and went in search of
food hoarded by speculators. Shouting of their hunger and in-
ability to pay inflated prices, they converged on the railroad
depot.

The railroad agent dissuaded them, saying that he had no
flour, and the mob turned to the store of "one of the oldest and
most respected citizens," where they broke into a warehouse,
and were given ten barrels of flour. Their next call was at a
nearby store, where they took seven barrels of flour; they then
broke into the government warehouse, which was empty.

On the street these women met a merchant reputed to be
speculating in salt, that rarest of staple commodities, but when
they hustled him to his storeroom, they found only one bag—
which they seized. Another storekeeper held them at bay with
the gift of a barrel of molasses, but the women, still dissatisfied,
returned to the railroad depot, and though the agent threatened
to die before allowing them to pass, the women stormed by him,
brandishing weapons. Here they rolled out ten barrels of flour.

A farmer who drove up with a wagonload of tobacco for

shipment was warned by the agent, and left behind running horses, "fearful that they would learn to chew and impress his tobacco."

This small town was the location of one of the most notorious of Confederate prisons, where thousands of Federal captives were held, amid growing protests that they were being starved. The civilian population found itself in little better straits.

Scarcely a fortnight later more serious trouble broke out in Richmond, where inflation and the extortioners had brought rocketing food prices. On April 2 a mob of about a thousand women and boys gathered in Capitol Square and streamed in ominous silence toward the retail district on Cary Street, breaking windows and looting stores of speculators as they went. The mob commandeered wagons and drays and piled them with loot, at first mostly meal, flour, and clothing.

A boy came from a store with a hatful of banknotes, and by the time the mob reached Main Street, shopkeepers had closed their doors. Windows and doors were smashed for blocks, and the attention of the women turned to jewelry, silks, and other luxuries. A troop of soldiers marched in, causing a temporary lull.

Richmond's mayor solemnly read the Riot Act to the looters and threatened to order the soldiers to fire if the mob did not disperse. The women were milling uncertainly when a tall, spare figure appeared: Jefferson Davis. The President climbed into a dray and begged the people to go to their homes, so that the troops might be sent to fight the enemy. He told them that looting could only intensify food shortages, and might cause famine, since farmers would cease bringing wagons to the city.

Davis said he was willing to share his last crust with the people—his horse and been stolen the night before—and he urged the crowd to bear its burdens bravely. The mob began to break up, and quiet at last came to the streets.

The President ordered censorship of the incident, and news was prevented from going out of the capital by telegraph, in the interest of public safety. But the Richmond *Enquirer* scolded the people two days later:

A handful of prostitutes, professional thieves, Irish and Yankee hags, gallows birds from all lands but our own, congregated in Richmond with a woman huckster at their head, who buys veal at the toll gate for 100 and sells the same for 250 in the morning market, undertook the other day to put into private practice the principles of the commissary department.

Swearing that they would have goods at government prices they broke open half a dozen shoe stores, hat stores and tobacco houses and robbed them of everything but bread, which was just the thing they wanted least.

Many Southern workmen struck for higher wages as prices spiraled upward. Men earning $3 per day while building the ironclad *Mississippi* in a New Orleans shipyard struck for a $4 wage in 1861, and persuaded twenty imported mechanics from Richmond to walk out with them. Yard owners met their demands, but a few of the ringleaders were jailed.

Richmond post office clerks struck for a raise, declaring that they were starving on salaries of $700 to $800 a year. Early in 1864 the Southern Telegraphic Association went on strike, seeking higher wages and fewer hours—not to mention a closed shop. The Typographical Society of Richmond had earlier made a vain effort in this direction. The strikes almost invariably failed. The Confederate Government quickly drafted those who left their jobs.

Abraham Lincoln faced more serious problems: In the last half of 1863, Illinois arrested over 2,000 deserters from the army, and Copperhead clubs, variously disguised as Knights of The Golden Circle, The Sons of Liberty, Order of American Knights and the like, swept the Western border states. Two draft officers were killed in Indiana, and in Pennsylvania one was shot and others were wounded, run from their homes, and burned out. The Pennsylvania coal country was paralyzed for months by the secret order, Molly Maguires, and owners of mines feared to report them to Washington because of threatened reprisals.

An entire Illinois regiment, the 109th, was arrested and

interned in Mississippi, when mutiny threatened. In January, 1863, Governor Morton of Indiana wired Lincoln that he expected his state legislature to recognize the Confederacy, and though the lawmakers did not go so far, they denied the State an appropriation, and Morton begged funds from Washington.

In early summer of '63 mobs surged through Chicago streets after soldiers seized the newspaper plant of the *Times*, under orders from General Burnside, and the unruly crowds threatened to sack the loyal Union *Tribune* in retaliation.

A measure of calm came when Lincoln banished the Copperhead leader, Clement Vallandigham—but even after his departure the Democrats of Ohio nominated the troublemaker for Governor.

19

The Inner Man

SOME historians say that the famed gallantry of Confederate infantry in charges under fire involved something more than sheer courage: hunger.

The half-starved gray-and-butternut files, gobbling their Rebel Yell at the tops of their voices, often carried fields because of their desire to rifle the full haversacks of the Federal troops—and to acquire new boots, uniforms, and arms.

Whatever the truth of this, Northern armies were almost always better fed, often to their own detriment as shock troops. Numerous observers noted the grisly differences in Confederate and Union dead on the battlefields. The Southern slain were white-faced and lean, much as in life; the Northern boys soon turned black and bloated. The singular variation was attributed to diet.

Soldiers on both sides complained bitterly of their rations, as in all wars. It was not always without reason, even in the well-supplied Union armies early in the war. After Shiloh, Grant's army was hard hit by diarrhea caused by poor food. Sutlers swarmed, as usual, and their prices were high: lemons, fifteen cents each; cheese, 40 cents a pound; whiskey, $1 per pint.

By the end of the war in conquered Richmond, inflation had become ruinous, with hens at $50 each, butter at $20 per pound, and fish $50 per pair.

Lack of food was perhaps the immediate cause of Lee's surrender; his army fell apart into bands of foragers after passing Amelia Court House on its way to Appomattox. The 350,000

rations expected there failed to arrive, and the inedible ordnance stores which replaced them were useless in the emergency.

General Lee probably had nothing to eat on the morning of Appomattox, and thousands of his men had no more than a few mouthfuls of boiled corn, stolen from the horses' rations. But the Confederate commander had lived like a Spartan throughout the war; meat came to his camp table but twice a week. When he captured many kegs of molasses on his invasion of Gettysburg, he set them aside for hospital use.

There were spectacular exceptions to the life of hardship.

When the Washington Artillery of New Orleans went to war it took along the chef of Victor's Restaurant, one Edouard, a character who kept a pet fox in camp, served the finest in French cuisine, but left the Confederate Army in disgust one day when his cooking utensils were sacrificed in a retreat.

A French count, as a volunteer officer with the Federal regiment, Gardes Lafayette, admired the delicious salad served in the headquarters mess.

"What meat is this?" he asked the cook one day. "I must take the recipe to France. It will be a sensation."

"Blacksnake," was the reply. The count paled, lost interest, and disappeared from the coterie of salad fanciers. The famed chef of the regiment was M. Soyer, abducted for the war from a New York restaurant.

General Blenker's troops in the Union service, mostly Germans, could not fight on white bread, and so got an extra allowance for the supply of rye and black bread from their own ovens. Beer was also an essential, and permission was granted to trundle barrels to their camps.

Business was so good that William Russell, writing for the London *Times*, reported that Blenker got from $6,000 to $8,000 monthly for granting beer licenses in his lines. A quartermaster officer seemed to have been the guilty party.

An authenticated case revealing the source of Confederate gallantry in action came from Colonel Len T. von Zincken of a Louisiana regiment, who in the midst of battle overheard a wounded Irishman cry to his comrades, "Charge 'em, boys! They have cheese in their haversacks!"

"Ersatz" in Confederate cookery contrasted with reported plenty, from the first days of the war. Captain Mercer Otey of the Signal corps reported chicken gumbo made of the tender twigs of sassafras, plus the "photograph of a long-gone chicken" —but pronounced the dish as excellent.

Champagne was made of three parts water and one part corn-and-molasses, fermented in an old molasses barrel. It lacked effervescence, but was popular in camp.

On St. Patrick's Day of 1863, in the lull before the campaign of Chancellorsville-Gettysburg, the Irish Brigade of the Union Army staged a celebration worthy of the occasion.

Quartermasters imported liquors and meat from Washington; they served thirty-five hams, half of an ox, chicken, duck, small game. The spectators enjoyed eight buckets of champagne, ten gallons of rum, twenty-two gallons of whiskey.

More than 30,000 men and women watched the Irish Sweepstakes for a $500 prize, with army riders on six famed horses going over ditches and hurdles. General Joseph Hooker watched as General Meagher's gray won—but this was followed by "Olympic Games," featuring greased pig races, wheelbarrow and sack races, and a tournament for Irish dancers.

In contrast, when General M. Jeff Thompson surrendered his small Confederate band in the Western theater, and Federal officers gave them rations, the men goggled in astonishment at such food as they had not seen in four years. Thompson reported the reactions of the men:

One pocket would be filled with salt, another with sugar, another with coffee; the hat with hard bread. They drank vinegar, put a bar of soap under one arm, and the bacon under the other, carrying the candles, rice, dried apples etc. as best they could in their hands.

The diet of Confederates in the field was movingly described by a Federal officer who found the slender body of a Tennessee boy, about fifteen, lying barefoot in the cold after the battle of Chattanooga. A day's rations were in his haversack: "A handful of black beans, a few pieces of sorghum and half a dozen roasted acorns."

Such soldiers were with Stonewall Jackson when he raided a Federal depot at Manassas Junction on the flanking march which opened the fighting of Second Manassas. Hungry men fell upon vast supplies of delicacies in a scene which was for many the most memorable of the war.

Pickled lobster and oysters in cans, barrels of coffee and flour, European wines and brandies and imported cigars—all were favorite spoils, described in detail by men who could not bring themselves to write thus of battle.

Confederate pride was wounded in an incident at Port Hudson on the Mississippi. As besieging Federals drew their lines tighter around the defenders, food became scarce. Southern quartermasters slaughtered mules to keep the troops alive, but, in hope of seeing reinforcements arrive almost any day, urged that the secret be kept from the enemy.

The Confederates knew that word of their sad plight had somehow filtered across the river when their blue-clad enemy appeared on the bank one morning, braying loudly in imitation of mules.

Southern troops were not always in such sore straits. In the days after the fall of Vicksburg, when "Major Purvis," a Scottish veteran of that siege, had become Quartermaster of the Sub-Department of Mississippi, statistics of supply were staggering.

Purvis once reported beginning at midnight the task of driving his crews to butcher and scald a thousand hogs for the next day's distribution to troops. His bakers turned out a thousand loaves of bread each day, at least for a brief period.

There is also the disquieting tale of one Joe Keno, a Frenchman who served as a Confederate cook, but grew weary of the chore and retired. He was saved from the role of combatant because of his foreign birth, but became a purveyor of fresh meat to army camps. He allegedly provided lamb and kid, but in truth, by camp rumor, the meat he brought for the sustenance of Southern valor was invariably dog.

20

Was Stonewall Jackson a Hypochondriac?

THE Confederate Lieutenant General, Thomas J. Jackson, one of the most gifted field commanders in American history, thought himself "out of balance," and even under fire in battle was given to raising one arm, and allowing the blood to flow down into his body and establish an equilibrium.

He refused to eat pepper, on the ground that it made his left leg weak. Despite wartime shortages, he often sucked lemons, believing that they helped his "dyspepsia." His staff officers noted his strange diet; some meals were made of raspberries, bread and milk.

Jackson was comfortable only when in a bolt upright position, with his organs held "naturally," one atop another. For this reason he had no chairs in his study at Lexington, Virginia, and spent hours standing at his reading of the Bible or memorizing of courses which he taught at Virginia Military Institute.

He took his second bride on a long tour of spas in Eastern America, taking steam baths, drinking and bathing in mineral waters and seeking to improve nagging bad health.

Even when he was a plebe at West Point, Jackson's complaints came to the notice of a first-classman, U.S. Grant, who recalled that Jackson was a "fanatic" whose delusions "took strange forms—hypochondria, fancies that an evil spirit had taken possession of him."

Jackson freely offered dietary advice to his sister, Laura, and once wrote: "If you commence on this diet, remember that it is like a man joining the temperance society; if he afterwards tastes liquor he is gone."

His complaints, issued almost endlessly through his young manhood, included: rheumatism, dyspepsia, chilblains, poor eyesight (which he was wont to treat by dipping his head into a basin of cold water, eyes open, for as long as he could hold his breath), cold feet, nervousness, neuralgia, impaired hearing, tonsillitis (which required an operation), biliousness, and "slight distortion of the spine."

As a result a theory has grown up that Jackson was a confirmed hypochondriac. But a modern physician says that he may well have suffered from a fairly common and most uncomfortable condition, diaphragmatic hernia. This is the surmise of Dr. E.R. MacLennan of Opp, Alabama, a veteran of general practice, civilian and military, based upon biographical reading on Jackson. A breach in the diaphragm, Dr. MacLennan points out, would produce symptoms of which Jackson complained for years without finding relief.

Whatever the trouble, war seems to have cured Jackson or to have diverted his attention. Aside from a written complaint to his wife that he suffered from "fever and debility" during the Seven Days battles, there is little on his medical record for the war years.

Ironically, Jackson's habit of draping his abdomen with cold towels in an effort to relieve pains of "dyspepsia" may have caused his death. He was wounded by his own men at Chancellorsville, recovered from the amputation of an arm, but after a servant placed cold towels on his body without the knowledge of attending physicians, Jackson contracted pleurisy and pneumonia, and died soon afterward.

Other aspects of Jackson's unusual personality served to emphasize his health problems. His stern, dedicated, withdrawn presence drew the scorn of VMI cadets and his wartime contemporaries—at first. Jackson kept his own counsel to such an extent that he once moved an army of about 25,000 men across complex terrain by instructing his generals to lead their troops from crossroad to crossroad—at each spot sending them further directions as to which road to take. His critics soon found that

his quirks concealed a military brain of surpassing brilliance—
one of the Confederacy's few really dependable weapons.

His tiny army of under 17,000 kept at bay four Federal
armies in the famed Shenandoah Valley campaign of 1862, and
finally defeated them, one by one, driving most of the 60,000-
odd bluecoats from Virginia and spreading terror in the North.

Jackson conducted some of the most daring flank attacks
in military history, and the prime example of this maneuver cost
him his life. At Chancellorsville, where he withdrew some 25,000
men from the main Confederate army, leaving Lee with few
more than 10,000 to face the enemy's 80,000, Jackson created
his masterpiece. He rolled up the Federal army and prepared it
for defeat, but was wounded a few moments after his triumph
became obvious.

Not the least of the oddities of Confederate legend created
by Jackson's wounding and death is a fully marked grave where
his left arm lies, in the graveyard of the Lacy family near Chancellorsville—probably the only one of its kind.

Jackson's military reputation is perhaps greater than that
of any other Civil War commander. He won it in twenty-two
months between First Manassas and Chancellorsville.

His career may have been foreshadowed in a little-known
incident from his first major battle: he was shot in the hand at
First Manassas, perhaps while holding up his arm in quest of
"body balance." After the fighting he sought a surgeon, who
said that the damaged finger must be amputated. The doctor
turned to find his instruments, and in that moment Jackson rode
away.

21

The Marvelous Ram Albemarle

THE shallow sounds indenting the North Carolina coast were Federal lakes in the spring of 1864. Large Yankee fleets pushed up the dark rivers inland. Nowhere was the blockade more effective.

In April came word of a Confederate menace: somewhere up the river Roanoke was a ship more terrible than the old converted *Merrimac*. She was daily expected to steam into the sound, scatter the invading fleet and break the blockade.

Federal sailors raised a barricade of sunken boats, pilings, and torpedoes in the river, bottling up the ram, for the barrier was as high as the greatest known tides.

The little Confederate navy spared nothing to make the *Albemarle* equal to her task. Chief Constructor John L. Porter designed her; Gilbert Elliott, a master builder, directed swarms of slaves and carpenters as she grew, and Captain J.W. Cooke, a veteran seaman, was her skipper. She was built at isolated Edwards Ferry on the Roanoke.

Her timbers were solid pine, 8 inches by 10; she was sheathed in 4-inch planks, and her raised octagonal shield, amidships, was 60 feet long, plated with 4 inches of iron. Her prow was an oaken beak, covered in iron, ground to the sharpness of a knife. She was 122 feet long, 45 feet in the beam, and drew 8 feet of water. She was driven by two engines of 400 horsepower.

She wallowed into the river on April 18, and after hesitating briefly at the enemy's barricade, went safely across in a record-breaking freshet, foiling the enemy. She ran head on into two formidable ships.

The *Miami*, a fast side-wheeler, was lashed by chains to the *Southfield*, a warlike ferryboat; the two charged in, trying to entrap the ram. These ships carried fifteen guns all told, one of them a huge 100-pounder.

Cooke played a crafty game. He veered for the shore of the river, and with a sudden turn opened his throttle and speared the *Southfield* broadside. The ferryboat sank with her crew, and the *Albemarle* wrenched free her beak only after some anxious moments when water was pouring into her hold.

The *Miami* was firing at close range, so close that a shell rebounded and killed the Federal captain. The *Miami* fled, leaving the ram the mistress of the Roanoke, unharmed and more threatening than ever.

The next morning, aided by the ram's guns, Confederate infantry recaptured the little town of Plymouth. A fortnight later, on May 5, the *Albemarle* invaded the sound whose name she bore, trailing behind her the captured steamer *Bombshell* and the river boat *Cotton Plant*, loaded with Rebel troops.

An enlarged Federal fleet closed with her, led by the *Miami*, which now bore a torpedo and a fouling net for the ram's propellers. The *Albemarle* went for the nearest ship, *Mattabesett*, and shot away her pivot rifle. Another enemy craft hit the *Albemarle* with a broadside of nine-inch shot. A Federal sailor watched in awe: "The guns might as well have fired blank cartridges, for the shot skimmed off into the air . . . even the 100-pound solid shot glanced from the sloping roof."

The Federals soon nipped off the *Bombshell* and forced her surrender. The enemy then halted engines and crowded their ships on either side of the ram, trying to hold her for the kill. Commander F.N. Rose of the *Sassacus* had waste rags and oil dumped into his boilers for maximum steam, and crashed his ship into the *Albemarle* while she was held tightly. The Confederate's lights went out, and she rolled, but her gun ports opened and a shell burst in the boiler of the *Sassacus*, scalding and blinding many men. A fight raged on the Federal ship's deck for about fifteen minutes as other bluecoats drifted, watching.

The *Miami*'s rudder was damaged, and she could not help *Sassacus*. A sister ship, the *Wyalusing*, sent a false message that she was sinking. The *Sassacus* drifted off the ram, having driven off Confederate boarders, and fired until the *Albemarle* limped out of range.

Now the effect of the big shot on the Rebel ship was even more striking to the watchful sailor: "The solid iron shot would bound from the roof into the air like marbles. Fragments even of our 100-pound rifle shots, at close range, came back on our own decks."

At dusk the ram steamed back up the Roanoke. She had not lifted the siege, but was intact, and might yet change the course of war. She went upriver to Plymouth, where she lay surrounded by a cordon of chained cypress logs, a protection against torpedo attack. She had a crew of sixty, but at least ten of these were usually on outpost duty, probing enemy lines. A picket was stationed on a schooner, anchored in the river about a gunshot from the ram—the only guard between the *Albemarle* and the enemy.

Lieutenant W.B. Cushing was already a legend in the Federal Navy, a night raider against North Carolina forts and towns. He proposed a desperate raid on the *Albemarle* to his superior, Admiral S.P. Lee (a kinsman of General R.E. Lee of the Confederacy). Cushing was sent to Washington and then to New York, in search of authority and weapons. Officers were dubious of his success.

He came South by sea with two open 30-foot launches, powered by tiny engines, each boat carrying a small gun and a boom for torpedoes. Cushing was supremely confident despite the odds. He lost one of the boats in coastal waters, but at last got the other into the Roanoke on the dark night of October 27, 1864. He towed a cutter filled with men, in order to deal with the Rebels on the picket boat if they were aroused.

Though he passed within thirty feet, there was no hail from the pickets, and Cushing puttered ahead, hoping that he could board the ram with his twenty men, who were armed with revolvers, cutlasses, and grenades.

They were within a few feet of the *Albemarle* when there
was a shout. Cushing cast off the cutter and made for the "dark
mountain of iron" at full speed. Shots rang out from shore, and
someone lit a bonfire. In the dim light Cushing saw the log boom
around the ram. He ran alongside her under fire, and veered
away to come back at right angles to the logs. He hoped that
the cypress had become slimy in the water and that his whaleboat would ease across. The back of his coat was torn away by
buckshot as he maneuvered, and the sole of one shoe was ripped
off.

An officer called from the *Albemarle*, "What boat is that?"
Cushing's men gave "comical answers" and the lieutenant replied
with a round of canister from his gun. The boat then struck the
logs and lurched over, within ten feet of the ram.

Cushing had his torpedo boom lowered, pulled a lanyard,
and thrust the explosive under the *Albemarle*. As she blew up,
his left hand was cut by a bullet and a storm of grape crashed
into the whaleboat. A massive geyser of water fell on the crew.

Cushing disregarded orders to surrender and told the crew to scatter. He shucked his coat, shoes, sword, and pistol, and left the sinking boat, swimming over the river as cannon and rifle fire splashed the water nearby. He was twelve miles from the safety of the Federal fleet.

Cushing could see Confederates in boats as they picked up survivors, and once heard his own name called. He was becoming feeble, swallowing water at each mechanical stroke of his arms. When he reached the muddy shore, he lay exhausted at the water's edge until daylight, and emerged half frozen. He found himself near a swamp just a few yards from a Rebel fort; strengthened by the warm sunshine he made a dash for some underbrush, but was forced to fall flat at the approach of a sentry. Rebel soldiers passed so near his mud-covered body that they almost stepped on him, and for five hours afterward Cushing squirmed toward the cover of the swamp, daring to move but a few inches each time.

Once inside the woodland, he struggled through a wilderness of thorns and vines that tore his skin, and often passed bogs so soft that he could not stand, and was forced to worm across at full length, pulling himself by his arms. His hands and feet were soon raw. He narrowly escaped a Rebel working party, and in the swamp met a Negro whom he bribed with twenty dollars and sent into Plymouth for news of the *Albemarle*.

The Negro was soon back with word that the ram was gone. Cushing plunged eastward into the swamps, stole a skiff from Confederate soldiers who were working a few yards away, and paddled down the river into Albemarle Sound. The waters were fortunately still, and the night clear and windless. Cushing steered by the stars for two hours and at last saw the outline of a vessel.

He hailed her and lay in cold water at the bottom of his skiff, worn out by ten hours of paddling. The picket vessel *Valley City* almost ended the tale in tragedy, for though her men heard Cushing's feeble cry, they would not pick him up, fearful of a Confederate ruse to launch a torpedo attack. The Federal sentries shouted back and forth across the water, questioning Cushing—who was thought to have died in the ram's explosion of the previous night. It was a long time before he was hauled aboard.

He drank a noggin of brandy and was sent toward the flagship. Rockets went up as word spread through the fleet, and men cheered from decks as he was rowed past. Before daybreak officers of the fleet were already in conference with Cushing on the flagship, planning an attack on Plymouth and the upper Roanoke, no longer defended by the *Albemarle*.

22

Some Oddities of This Odd War

IF the Civil War had a champion soldier, he must have been George Barnhart Zimpleman, of Terry's Texas Rangers CSA, a private by choice, who went through more than 400 battles and skirmishes up to May, 1865, led his regiment in the number of horses shot from under him, and suffered two wounds, one of which maimed him for life.

Federal ordnance men turned down the Spencer repeating breech-loading rifle in 1860, and did not get it into the hands of troops in quantity until near the end of the war. The theory for their refusal: Soldiers would fire too fast, and waste ammunition.

Firing on both sides was so inaccurate that soldiers estimated it took a man's weight in lead to kill a single enemy in battle.

A Federal expert said that each Confederate who was shot required 240 pounds of powder and 900 pounds of lead.

One of the war's most striking victories was won by an Irishman in Confederate service, Captain Richard W. Dowling, nineteen, of the Davis Guards. With 43 men armed with rifles and six small cannon he defended Sabine Pass, Texas, in September, 1863, driving off a Federal fleet which tried to land about 15,000 men.

Dowling sank one gunboat, disabled and captured two others, and turned away the rest of the fleet. He took 400 prisoners—all without the loss of a man.

This was the only command of record in the war to get its

whole muster roll into official reports. All the men got silver medals from Jefferson Davis, the only such given by the Confederacy.

A Monsieur Chillon, a French army veteran who had migrated to California, walked cross-country to war in 1861, through Indian territory accompanied only by his donkey, Jason, with whom he slept.

Chillon was welcomed by the French-speaking 3rd Louisiana of the Confederate Army and settled down. There was one trouble: the regiment's colonel bore a strong resemblance to old Chillon, and at bedtime Jason invariably pushed into the commander's tent and tried to curl up next to the officer, to the joyous yelping of the troops.

Of the future members of the United States Supreme Court who were of fighting age during the war, seven were in uniform. Four fought for the Union: Oliver Wendell Holmes, John M. Harlan, William B. Woods, and Stanley Matthews. Three fought for the Confederacy: Edward D. White, Horace H. Lurton, and Lucius Q.C. Lamar.

Two of the war's most famous, and bloody, battles may be said to have been fought because of trifles. Gettysburg, because a few soldiers needed shoes, and their column was sent to that Pennsylvania village for them. Sharpsburg, or Antietam, because a Confederate officer wrapped three cigars with a vital army order, and carelessly dropped or discarded them. This order, found by a Federal soldier, enabled the usually cautious General McClellan to attack Lee's divided army.

The 8th Wisconsin regiment had one of the most remarkable mascots in the Union armies: Old Abe, a lively eagle. Abe had been brought to war by a soldier who had traded for the bird with an Indian on the frontier, in exchange for five bushels of corn. In camp, the bird followed his master like a puppy.

In battle Abe invariably soared aloft until the shooting stopped, and then returned to the 8th Wisconsin. He feared

artillery fire, and flew so high during engagements that he was almost lost to sight, and had the only bird's-eye view of most battles in the Western theater. He sustained at least one wound, but survived to live for fifteen years in the Wisconsin State House, and today, a gem of the taxidermist's art, is on display in the Wisconsin State Museum.

Two brothers, Jack and Jasper Walker, of Charlotte, North Carolina, fought at Gettysburg with the 13th North Carolina. Jasper, the younger, was wounded on July 1, as the fifth color-bearer of his regiment to be shot. A surgeon amputated his leg. Jasper was captured and sent to a Northern prison.

On the retreat from Gettysburg, Jack Walker was also shot and lost his left leg by amputation. He went to another Federal prison.

The brothers returned home after the war to become prosperous citizens, familiar in the town as they stumped about on cork legs. On Jasper's wedding day, when he accidentally fell and broke his artificial limb, he borrowed the leg of his gallant brother—a perfect fit.

This, as Confederate veterans were fond of telling youngsters, was the only case on record in which one man was married while standing on the leg of another.

Though more than 27,000 were casualties of the battle of Chickamauga, and 4,000 were killed, only one soldier is known to lie on the field today.

He is Private John Ingraham, of the 1st Confederate Regiment, Georgia Volunteers, an orphan who was buried by comrades where he fell and remained there despite removal of all other known bodies in development of the battlefield park.

Sergeant Henderson Virden of the 2nd Arkansas went to war at the advanced age of twenty-five, and for a year had no word from his wife and children, back in Pea Ridge. In March, 1862, he found himself marching through familiar country, and was soon fighting across his own farm in the battle of Pea Ridge, or Elkhorn Tavern.

Virden was wounded and carried into his own house, where his wife tended him until he could return to his regiment. During his convalescence Mrs. Virden conceived a son, Wiley, who became the father of eight children. The youngest of this third generation, Colonel John M. Virden, was in 1960, as the Centennial of the war approached, one of the country's most devout Confederates, and an editor of military service newspapers in Washington, D.C., after a wartime career with Claire Chenault's Flying Tigers and a hitch as press-relations man for General Eisenhower at SHAPE headquarters in Paris.

Grandpa Virden lived to be ninety-three, with a Yankee Minié ball under the skin of his back and a huge white scar on his chest.

A young Confederate officer, Captain S. Isadore Guillet, was fatally shot on the same horse on which three of his brothers had been previously killed. He willed the animal to a nephew as he died.

Some Mexican companies of the Confederate armies gained a reputation for unreliability. Private Juan Ivra was not of this stripe. In one Western action he staged a one-man charge into the faces of forty astonished Federals, and forced them to flee.

One Claude Pardigon, a Frenchman en route to join the Southern cause, challenged the skipper of a blockade-runner to a duel because he did not provide toothbrushes for passengers.

Paul A. Fusz, who enlisted as a Confederate private in 1861 at the age of fifteen, was caught with two other soldiers smuggling quinine through the Federal lines. The smugglers chewed up their papers, but their captors shot the older two. The tradition is that the pardoning of Fusz was Lincoln's last official act.

A nameless German soldier with the Army of Northern Virginia lived like a hermit in every camp, and in winter hibernated like a primitive man in a hut of leaves and brush, living a life apart. His language was unintelligible, and he is said to have served through the war without exchanging an understandable word with his fellows.

Major Robert Anderson, the Union commander at Fort Sumter as the war opened, was a former slave-owner. He at first found himself at old Fort Moultrie in Charleston Harbor— a spot where his father had served before him, in the Revolution.

Slaves in Virginia could be hired for $30 a month in 1863 —yet the pay of an Army private was $11 per month. Confederate pay rose to $18 per month the next year.

Union privates drew only $16, but the gold value of their pay was more than seven times greater than that of Confederates.

John M. Ozanne, a French sharpshooter in the Southern Army, became a true hero to those in gray by resigning his lieutenant's commission in protest, saying that he could not buy food and clothing on his small pay. The resulting change in the law provided supplies for officers.

Despite the neat phrase which has come down to us, "The Blue and the Gray," uniforms of the armies were fantastically varied, and often perplexing:

When the war opened, Federal troops were often clad in "Standard Gray." The 3rd New York, the 1st Vermont and almost all Indiana troops wore gray with black facings—just as did Confederate troops from Georgia.

The 1st Iowa dressed like troops from Louisiana. Men of Maine, Kansas, and Nebraska wore gray.

A New Jersey battalion of cavalry wore blue and yellow, and was known as "The Butterflies." A Polish regiment from New York wore traditional native caps, square, and blazing in red and white.

The Union Army had one company made up entirely of pugilists. There were others composed of musicians, farmers, or butchers. One Temperance Company went into battle stone sober, tradition has it. The 126th New York was the YMCA Regiment. Nicholas Busch, later Lieutenant Governor of Iowa, formed a woodchoppers' corps of German immigrants who were unable to fight, and had them cut and haul wood for Mississippi River army steamers—pausing now and then to beat off guerrillas.

Secretary of War Simon Cameron, a Pennsylvania politician in Lincoln's Cabinet, opposed early orders for European rifles, saying that these should be bought at home—and that the North already had too many guns for the men at hand. One result: The Confederates were able to reach some markets first, and import arms they would otherwise have lost.

In the Confederate retreat as the battle of Shiloh ended, three gray-clad officers rode past Colonel A.K. Johnson, of the 28th Illinois regiment. Johnson chased and fired at one rider. The victim slumped on his horse's neck, but Johnson, thinking this a feint, rode nearer and seized the Confederate by the hair to drag him from the saddle. A tug brought him a trophy—a wig. The Confederate officer was dead, and soon toppled to the ground.

Early in the war, when Confederate invasion of Washington was threatened, field guns were placed in hallways of the Capitol and Treasury building.

The iron plates cast for the dome of the Capitol were raised on heavy timbers between columns of the building as breastworks. Statuary and pictures were shielded with heavy planking, and an army kitchen was set up in the basement.

The fearsome Confederate ironclad ram *Arkansas* dueled the Federal gunboat *Carondelet* at the mouth of the Yazoo River in July, 1862. Northern courage and Southern ingenuity produced a drawn battle. The ram could not be damaged by shells, and the Federal boat, when shot through by cannon fire, drew alongside the *Arkansas* and sent a boarding party onto the decks of the ram.

Once there, the daring Yankees were at a loss—for the ram's crew merely retired below decks, slammed the iron hatches after them, and left no one to fight. A stalemate resulted.

The Confederate General, Nathan Bedford Forrest, classed by some historians as the war's most able cavalry commander, had twenty-nine horses shot from under him in the course of the war. He survived to become a founder of the Ku Klux Klan.

The town of Winchester, Virginia, changed hands seventy-six times during the war, as the armies surged to and fro in the Northern Shenandoah Valley.

There was an Abraham Lincoln on each side in the war. The President, and a Confederate, Private Abraham Lincoln of Company F, 1st Virginia Cavalry, from Jefferson County. He was reported as a deserter in 1864, so that the North ended with both.

Years before the war Jesse Grant, father of Ulysses, lived and worked in the home of Owen Brown, whose small son, playing noisily about the frontier homestead, grew up to be John Brown, the Abolitionist martyr who lit the fuse of the war.

After the war many Confederate officers fled to foreign countries rather than live in the reunited republic; some 3,000 went to Brazil alone, in an ill-fated effort to build a prosperous new life.

A striking contrast was the North Carolinian, Dick Ragland, a man of a wealthy plantation family who swore an oath, upon hearing of Lee's surrender, that he would not lift a finger to work so long as he lived.

Ragland also vowed that he would never cross to the north side of the Potomac, or stray south of Atlanta, Georgia. Until after 1910 he tramped the South as a vagrant, shaggy and ragged, with a pack on his back, carrying a long stick with a bayonet fixed on its end.

The first Confederate general to be killed was Robert S. Garnett, shot at Corrick's Ford, Virginia, before the first battle of Manassas/Bull Run. He was first buried in Baltimore, then secretly moved to a Brooklyn cemetery plot beside his wife. His identity was not revealed by the family because of strong wartime sectional feeling. His resting place remained generally unknown until 1959.

The youngest Confederate general was William Paul Roberts of North Carolina, a cavalry commander who went to war at twenty. His claim to the title has been established only recently through a study of vital statistics.

Of the 425 Confederate generals, 77 were killed or died of wounds during the war. The last surviving lieutenant general of the Southern armies was Simon Bolivar Buckner, who lived until 1914; his son and namesake was killed as a general in World War II.

Joseph E. Johnston, the "dean" of Confederate generals, who was jealous of his seniority, lost his hair from an illness, and wore a hat at table during the war, to the undisguised amusement of his servants.

Under the terms of Johnston's surrender to Sherman near Durham, North Carolina, many more men were surrendered than Lee gave up at Appomattox.

In postwar years Johnston served as pallbearer for several prominent Union generals, including U.S. Grant. His last such service was for William T. Sherman, his conqueror. While paying his respects to Sherman in the cemetery on a raw winter day, Johnston contracted a severe cold which became pneumonia and caused his death.

Eight Federal generals came from the small town of Galena, Illinois (15,000 population). They probably owed their rank to their friendship with U.S. Grant, the most celebrated wartime citizen of the place.

The list included John Aaron Rawlins, who was Grant's chief of staff; the Seneca Chief, Ely S. Parker, an engineer who became Grant's secretary and postwar commissioner of Indian Affairs; Jasper Maltby, a gunsmith said to have been the inventor of a telescopic sight; and Augustus L. Chetlain, a storekeeper who became Consul to Brussels and a leading Chicago banker.

The "biggest man-made explosion in history" was planned for the demise of the ship *Louisiana,* set adrift with 215 tons of fused powder in an effort to destroy Fort Fisher, near Wilmington, North Carolina. The scheme, conceived by General Benjamin Butler, failed because of poor fuses, and "The H-Bomb Of The Civil War" became a dud.

When Fort Fisher was finally taken by Federal forces, a Confederate prisoner, queried as to the effect of the big blast, said, "It was horrible. Woke up every man in the fort."

The ship actually went up, piecemeal, on a sand bar at some distance from the fort, causing no damage.

Mrs. Bridget ("Irish Biddy") Divers, wife of a private of the 1st Michigan Cavalry, won fame in the war by standing picket duty day and night, riding on raids against the Rebels, and taking the places of officers in emergencies. She once rode twelve miles to reclaim the body of a captain, and brought it into camp on horseback, having been passed by the Confederates because of her sex.

Biddy served as a nurse and surgeon, and was familiar to thousands of troops, a stout, leathery faced little woman with bleached hair and a cheery disposition. In at least one instance, in the battle of Fair Oaks/Seven Pines, she rallied a retreating Federal regiment and took it back into action.

Of 546 nuns known to have served as battlefield nurses, 289 were from Ireland, 40 from Germany, 12 from France.

After the fall of Norfolk and Portsmouth, Virginia, the Confederate Navy Yard was moved to a spot more than two hundred miles inland, at Charlotte, North Carolina. For three years it produced cannon balls, iron masts, and other fleet supplies.

John Ericsson, the genius who produced the *Monitor*, was forced to build his ship with private capital, some $275,000 in all —and was to be reimbursed by the Federal Government only if it were effective against the Confederate ironclad *Merrimac*, or *Virginia*.

The *Monitor* was modeled after Swedish lumber rafts Ericsson had known in his youth; its deck was only two inches above water. An effort to sell the idea of such a ship to Napoleon III failed, but the French did order five ironclad ships, despite the reputation of the inventor as a crank.

General Lloyd Tilghman, a Confederate killed in action at Champion Hill, just before Vicksburg, is said by even the most recent and authoritative reference works to be buried in Vicksburg. He is actually buried in Woodlawn Cemetery, New York City, his body having been moved there in 1901.

Chimborazo Hospital, in Richmond, is said to have been the largest hospital ever built in the Western Hemisphere, and to hold that distinction to this day.

23

Spies at Work

ON the morning of September 1, 1864, a Confederate soldier, strolling on the beach near Wilmington, North Carolina, found the body of a middle-aged woman. He opened a bag which lay beside her and saw the glint of gold—$2,000 in coin. He pushed the body back into the surf and hurried away, a man of means.

The body soon floated to another point, and was identified as that of the Confederacy's fabled spy, Rose O'Neal Greenhow. She had drowned while trying to make shore in a small boat from a blockade-runner, at the end of a voyage from England. The patriotic soldier who had robbed her was so touched by the news that he gave up his money to officials and joined the mourners. Mrs. Greenhow was buried in a Wilmington cemetery; it was a fittingly strange end for a singular career.

Rose had been queen of Washington society in the Buchanan administration, and for her intimacy with the President the subject of gossip; she was connected by marriage to the family of Stephen A. Douglas. When old John Calhoun died in her aunt's boardinghouse, Rose heard him muttering predictions of civil war with his last breath. When war came, she turned immediately to espionage.

Her great coup gave the Confederates accurate word of Union army movements before the Battle of Bull Run/Manassas. She sent a message through the lines rolled in the hairdo of pretty Betty Duvall, one of her agents, telling General Beauregard that the Union troops were marching. After passing inferior officers with some difficulty, Betty unrolled her hair before a Confederate general, dramatically producing a dispatch which took its place in history. A few days later Mrs. Greenhow added details, predicting the route of march of General Irvin McDowell's men. She did much to help the South win the first great battle.

Rose was prone to boast of her achievements as a spy, and this may have led the tenacious Federal agent, Allen Pinkerton, to her door. He found evidence that placed her in Old Capitol Prison—by odd circumstance the building her aunt had once used as a boardinghouse, and where Calhoun had died. Even in prison Mrs. Greenhow was defiant, and active as a spy during her four-month stay.

For some reason she sought to implicate Senator Henry Wilson of Massachusetts as an accomplice, and allowed Federal officials to find packets of love letters from Wilson, evidently forgeries. (Wilson became Vice President in 1873.)

Mrs. Greenhow was released, went to Richmond in triumph, and was given $2,500 by the Confederate secret service to operate as an agent in Europe. She spent much time there writing and publishing her memoirs, which were successful as Confederate propaganda.

An even more dramatic role was played by Belle Boyd, the *femme fatale* of Confederate agents. She began, at the age of seventeen, with the murder of a Federal soldier who raised a United States flag over her home in Martinsburg, Virginia. She went through a dizzy routine of arrest and imprisonment, helped Turner Ashby and Stonewall Jackson win the Shenandoah Valley Campaign of 1862, and vamped men on either side, in wholesale fashion.

Romance led Belle into and out of trouble; one sweetheart, C.W.D. Smitley, a West Virginia cavalryman, betrayed her into Old Capitol Prison. She made history there by furiously assailing the Federal detective chief, Lafayette Baker, when he urged her to sign a loyalty oath to the Union:

"I hope that when I commence that oath, my tongue may cleave to the roof of my mouth. If I ever sign one line to show allegiance, I hope my arm falls paralyzed to my side. . . . Get out. I'm so disgusted I can't endure your presence any longer."

Baker retreated. Belle remained there, living like an empress, reading fashionable magazines and eating delicacies brought by sympathizers. She sang one line from "My Maryland"—"She spurns the Northern scum"—with such fervor that her guards rushed into her cell to halt her singing. When they emerged, she furiously swept the cell behind them. She left a prison romance behind at her release and went to Richmond as a heroine; the jilted prison superintendent sent after her a trousseau he had bought for her himself.

Belle was trapped on a blockade-runner captured by a Federal ship, but so charmed a young ensign on the enemy vessel that he proposed. Belle embroiled him in Confederate espionage, and when he was discovered and dismissed from the United States Navy she sailed to England. The ex-ensign, Sam Hardinge, followed, and they were married in London, setting a high mark for the social season.

Hardinge returned to America and was jailed as a Southern spy. He died soon after the end of the war, and the widow, a charming twenty-one, turned to writing her memoirs and lecturing. She appeared in British and American theaters and on lecture platforms until 1900. She is buried in Wisconsin, beneath a stone proclaiming her as a Confederate spy.

Many spies of the war are little known today. One of the most engaging was Miss S. Emma E. Edmonds, a young Canadian nurse who was so skilled as a rider and marksman that she foraged as a hunter, providing meat for her patients.

She was also an impersonator of some ability, and during the fighting around Yorktown, early in 1862, disguised herself as a Negro man, worked for several days in Confederate lines, and brought back detailed information on Southern defenses and plans. She also discovered a counterspy.

In a disguise as a soldier, she became "Frank Thompson," and during the Seven Days battles was an orderly to General Phil Kearny. In Pope's campaign in Northern Virginia she made three visits into enemy lines, penetrating Confederate headquarters and learning many secrets.

After the battle of Antietam/Sharpsburg, when she was riding with a cavalry company, she was wounded when Confederates overwhelmed the column. A horse was killed under her, but she escaped.

At Fredericksburg, under heavy fire much of the day, she served as an aide to General Hancock.

At last, while serving with the Western armies, Emma wounded a Confederate captain who attempted to conscript her. She then left the field, deciding that it was too dangerous.

Emma became a detective for the Union in St. Louis, which was teeming with Rebel spies, and was responsible for spotting many of their activities.

Her adventures are recorded in a lively book, *Unsexed, or the Female Soldier.*

An interesting spy, or "mail carrier," was Charles Heidsick, a scion of the still-famous French champagne family, who was caught in New Orleans when war came. He was engaged in collecting delinquent accounts for his firm, but soon turned to more exciting work.

Disguised as a bartender, Heidsick worked on several Mississippi steamers and carried information through the lines for the Confederacy. General Benjamin Butler caught him, and was on the point of hanging him when Washington intervened.

Dr. William T. Passmore, an Englishman, was used as a spy by Robert E. Lee in the late fall of 1862. The doctor, dressed in rags and pretending to be a half-wit, wandered through the camps of General Burnside, selling produce from a cart. His disguise was so effective that Burnside gave him a pass for daily entry into Federal lines, and talked freely in front of him at headquarters. Passmore was credited with discoveries which enabled Lee to make plans leading to victory at Fredericksburg.

Antonia Ford, the pretty daughter of a storekeeper in Fairfax, Virginia, is also said to have helped Confederates win the battle of First Manassas, with information she picked up behind Union lines. This spy acted informally, and little of her routine work is known.

General J.E.B. Stuart did give her a commission in October, 1861:

> Know ye: that reposing special confidence in the patriotism, fidelity and ability of Miss Antonia Ford, I, James E.B. Stuart, by virtue of the power vested in me, as Brigadier General in the Provisional Army of the Confederate States of America, do hereby appoint and commission her my honorary aide-de-camp, to rank as such from this date.
>
> She will be obeyed, respected and admired by all the lovers of a noble nature. . . .

Almost two years later the miniature guerrilla leader, Colonel John S. Mosby (he weighed 125 pounds in the saddle), used Antonia as a spy. With her aid he snatched General E.H. Stoughton from headquarters, abducting him, several other Federal officers, and eighty-five horses, without so much as firing a shot.

The resulting clamor in Washington sent Lafayette Baker into action: He sent a woman agent to Fairfax, posing as a Southern sympathizer. The two women became friendly, and Antonia revealed her "commission" from Stuart and told her other Confederate secrets. Baker took Antonia prisoner and jailed her in Washington. Romance interfered.

Antonia's sweetheart was Major Joe Willard, USA, of the Washington hotel family. He wangled a transfer from the field to the prison department in Washington, to be near his betrothed. Antonia's granddaughter, Mrs. Kermit Roosevelt, has said that family tradition insists it was Joe himself who accompanied Antonia from her Fairfax home to prison.

In any event, Antonia signed a loyalty oath to the Union in 1863 before Major Joe Willard, and the pretty spy thereafter passed between Fairfax and Washington almost at will. In return for her pledge to give up spying for the Confederacy, Joe Willard resigned from the United States Army, and they were married.

24

The Gettysburg Address

MR. LINCOLN was suffering from a fresh case of smallpox when he delivered the most famous speech in American history. It was not diagnosed until he had made his brief appearance and rode back to Washington from Gettysburg. It was a mild case, as it happened, but the President felt ill on the train journey, and lay with a wet cloth across his brow, seeking relief.

The address accumulated legends from the start, many of them false, like the tale that Lincoln wrote his speech on an envelope as he jostled along the rails to Gettysburg.

David Wills, a Gettysburg lawyer, was chairman of the town's committee to create a national cemetery on the edge of the great battlefield. Two months before the ceremony he wrote the renowned orator, Edward Everett, asking him to make the address. Not until two weeks before the event did Lincoln get an invitation, and was then given limits that promised little for the occasion. Wills wrote:

> It is the desire, that after the oration, you, as chief executive of the nation, formally set apart these grounds to their sacred use by a few appropriate remarks.

Lincoln wrote at least one page of the first draft of the speech in Washington, on White House stationery, on November 17, 1863. He added the final nine and a half lines, in pencil, when he went to his bedroom in the Gettysburg home of David Wills the following evening.

On the morning of the address, November 19, Lincoln wrote a new draft, copying the first, and making few changes.

There were 239 words in the first and 269 words in the second draft.

Students were soon to pore over this address, analyzing it to the last comma, and despite disparities caused by numerous copies, made statistics based on its words:

Five words of the address were one-letter words (all of them the letter "a"). Forty-six had two letters, forty-four had three, fifty-six had four, thirty had five, twenty-five had six, thirteen had seven, and the rest eight or more letters. There were only eighteen words of three or more syllables.

Lincoln left the Wills House for the ceremonies at 10 A.M., riding horseback in a military parade. He sat on a crowded platform facing an audience of some 15,000, a bit restless, companions noted, as Everett intoned a two-hour oration. The President wore glasses when he rose, his little speech in hand. He glanced at the paper but once or twice and was on his feet less than three minutes, delivering the ten chiseled sentences in his high, squeaky voice.

If anyone recognized the greatness of the speech at the moment he is lost to history. Audience and dignitaries expressed private disappointment, and most newspapers ignored it, or gave it harsh treatment.

The following day, however, Everett wrote Lincoln:

> Permit me to express my admiration. . . . I would be glad if I could flatter myself that I came as near the central idea of the occasion in two hours, as you did in two minutes.

Lincoln made a gracious reply:

> In our respective parts yesterday, you could not have been excused to make a short address, nor I a long one. I am pleased to know that, in your judgment, the little I did say was not entirely a failure.

The first real applause came from the *Tribune* of Chicago, which said that the speech would "live in the annals of man."

The Address began to acquire value in the market place early in 1864. At the request of Everett, who was prompted by

Mrs. Hamilton Fish of New York, Lincoln made a copy of the speech and sent it to the Metropolitan Fair in New York, to be sold for charity. Lincoln inserted two words which every newspaper had quoted him as using, but which were not in the original draft: "under God." It is uncertain whether Lincoln actually spoke these words.

The Metropolitan Fair sold to a Mr. Keyes of New Hampshire its copies of Everett's and Lincoln's speeches—for $1,000.

Lincoln later made two more such copies for the historian, George Bancroft, to be sold at a Baltimore fair. The first of these copies was not auctioned because the President failed to sign it. The second one received some editing by Lincoln, who changed the punctuation slightly, and at one point omitted the word "here."

Of these five known copies, experts report, three have been sold commercially several times, for a total of $605,000, an average rate of about $2,225 per word, said to be the highest price ever brought by written words.

The Wills House still stands in Gettysburg, a museum dedicated to Lincoln's brief visit and speech.

25

The Hero of Gettysburg

JOHN BURNS was a village character, a sometime constable and cobbler who said he was descended from the Scottish poet, Bobbie; a hard-drinking old man who had fought in the War of 1812 and the Mexican War. If the Rebels came as far as Gettysburg, he told the townspeople, he'd show them how an old soldier could fight.

John was past seventy in July of '63, and no one could take seriously his talk of fighting. He had been too long the butt of village jokes.

He had once walked the ten miles from his home in Bendersville, saying that he'd heard there would be an eclipse of the moon, and that he had come to town in order to see it.

He had been baited by friends because he grumbled about "secret societies," and when he hurled insults at a meeting of Odd Fellows, the conspirators feigned anger and chased him wildly down a street.

Yet Burns had tried to volunteer at the first call to arms in this war, and when refused had gone to West Chester to enlist in the reserves. When he was again turned away, he went to Washington and served for a time as a driver in the wagon service.

On the morning of July 1, when the sounds of opening battle crackled in Gettysburg, Old John put on his Sunday best, a swallow-tailed blue coat with gilt buttons and a tall bell-crowned hat. Deaf to the scolding of his wife he left his home and fell in the ranks of a passing regiment, the 150th Pennsylvania Volun-

teers. He took a musket from a wounded man at the roadside and hurried toward the front.

Colonel Langhorne Wister of the 150th stared when Burns asked if he could join the fight.

"Can you shoot?"

"Give me a chance and I'll show you who can shoot."

Wister sent Burns from his position in the open to a woodland where part of the Iron Brigade was in line. One of the soldiers left a memory of it:

"We joshed him unmercifully. Some of the boys called him 'Daddy' and laughed at him, but he took it well. Then when he started firing we seen that this here old man knew how to handle a gun."

One of Burns's shots appeared to have knocked a Confederate officer from his horse, and troops of the 7th Wisconsin cheered; some of them gave Burns a silver-chased rifle they had captured from the Rebs, as a trophy.

The old man was struck by a bullet on his belt buckle; the fierce blow doubled him up, and he disappeared from the view of the front-line men of the Iron Brigade. He got two slight wounds, one a painful cut on an ankle which disabled him. As Confederate infantry approached him, John buried his rifle, or scurried away from it, and crawled onto the door of a cellar in the village.

A Rebel doctor treated his wounds. By one tradition, still a favorite with some Park historians, John hailed a passerby: "Tell my old woman to fetch the wagon and get me home. I can't move."

The wife's reported reply: "Devil take him. The old fool, going off to fight, as old as he is, getting holes in his best clothes. And he won't be able to work for two months. Let him stay."

Suddenly, John was a celebrity. General Abner Doubleday, "the baseball man," praised him in his report of the battle and the old soldier became known as "The Hero of Gettysburg." This was a distant fame, however, and his stature at home was little changed. A few poets set him to rhyme, including Bret Harte, who immortalized him in caricature.

Four months later when Lincoln came to town for the most famous of his addresses, the master politician asked to see John Burns. The bewildered townspeople were treated to the sight of the long-legged Lincoln arm in arm with the stubby Burns, who trotted to keep the pace along Chambersburg Street, around the Square and out Baltimore Street to the Presbyterian Church, a strange destination for Burns.

He later became a member of the church, and today is celebrated by a bronze plaque there. John drew his Civil War and other pensions for a few years and died in February, 1872. He left an estate of $13.25 in personal effects, a value of $1,518 in his forty-six acres of land, and a box of books, in which was found twenty-five cents.

He is buried in Evergreen Cemetery at Gettysburg, beneath a statue depicting him facing the Rebels with a musket. His wife lies at his side.

26

Sex in the Civil War

IN May, 1862, while Stonewall Jackson was becoming a military immortal in the Shenandoah Valley and Robert E. Lee was assuming command of the Army of Northern Virginia, a complaint was filed with the Richmond provost marshal.

The manager of the soldiers' hospital operated by the Young Men's Christian Association protested that he was being thwarted by Vice. Just across the street a shrewd madam had opened a resort of ill repute, and convalescent patients were being openly summoned by half-dressed women in her windows. There was a brisk cross-street pedestrian traffic.

By the opening of the Seven Days battles that spring, Richmond was so overrun with women of the streets that newspapers complained decent people could not use the sidewalks. Confederate officers paraded with these painted women on their arms so frequently that it became a public scandal, furiously denounced in the press.

Letters from soldiers reveal the presence of armies of prostitutes in most sections of the South, and many of these warned homefolks, especially wives and female relatives, to shun army camps because of the trollops who had quarters nearby.

The modern reader will find little of this spicy lore unless he persists, for though the men of 1861–65 were frequently outspoken, their relatives and descendants in postwar Victorian days became impassioned censors who weeded out most signs of the bawdy life of war years.

When General Hooker took command of the Army of the Potomac, his realistic policy toward recreation for the troops

changed Washington overnight. Red-light districts flourished.
Tradition strongly insists that it was this benevolent commanding
general who gave his name to the slang expression "hooker,"
signifying both an abandoned woman and a drink of whiskey,
neat.

Records are incomplete, especially on the Confederate side,
but even so the sins of the times are unmistakably documented:

The Union Army Medical Department reported in 1861
that 1 out of 12 soldiers had venereal disease, an almost incredible rate.

The Federal rate for the war was 82 cases per 1,000 men.

One report, covering white Union troops with a mean
strength of about 468,000 men, shows 188,000 cases of venereal
disease. Of 63,000 Negro Union troops, over 14,000 were dis-
eased.

In July, 1861, an official report on a dozen Confederate regiments with a strength of about 11,000, showed 204 new cases of
gonorrhea and forty-four of syphilis. In the next three months,
among larger bodies of troops, there were 572 new cases of the
diseases.

One Confederate artillery battery once reported 13 of its 45
men hospitalized with venereal disease.

Not only were both armies followed by large parties of
women, but both reported several cases of women who disguised
themselves as men, often dispensing their favors widely before
being detected and banished.

Despite a barrage of Southern wartime propaganda, there
are few recorded acts of sexual violence by Negroes during the
war, though some cases are known.

On June 20, 1864, the Union army hanged a convicted
Negro rapist of a white woman within plain view of Confederate
lines before Petersburg. The aim was propagandistic, since Provost Marshal General Marsena R. Patrick hoped to convince the
enemy that such criminals would be brought to justice.

The incident was cleverly turned to advantage by the Confederates, who had been losing hundreds of Negro laborers by
desertion. The Rebels marched Negroes past the spot, pointing

out to them the peril of fleeing their lines, saying that the Yankees hanged all "Contrabands." For weeks nocturnal escapes of Negroes ceased on that front.

Despite this stern example two white soldiers of the Union Army were tried for rape at Petersburg hardly a month later, and convicted after a stout defense, which made it appear that they had merely visited an informal bordello behind the siege lines. Recent directives from Generals Grant and Meade had insisted that the sanctity of the home be respected, even the Rebel home, and in conformity with the new policy the two men were strung up before a large soldier audience. General Patrick made a stirring address, asking men to remember their mothers, sisters, and daughters, while they gazed at the swinging bodies of the unfortunates.

In a postscript to this case, the Southern woman who had accused these men of rape (they were soldiers of the 72nd New York) confessed on her deathbed years after the war that she "swore the lives of these men away in order to contribute her mite toward the extermination of the Yankee army."

An occasional lively lady caused a rumpus on the home front, as a Miss Anna Lang did one day in Washington. Anna, far gone in drink, removed her clothing, except for shoes and stockings, and gave it to a teamster to wash. She hid in the bushes but soon tired of that and appeared in public, where she won an appreciative and noisy audience of young men. The police drove off her admirers and took Anna into custody—with much difficulty. They could not keep a blanket on her and when they called an ambulance the officers were forced to carry her by hands, legs, and head; she tore the uniforms from several policemen in the process. A judge fined her two dollars and Anna was soon on her way to the army camps, where she was much at home. She had already served a year and a half as "a soldier."

In addition, of course, were currents of rumor and gossip North and South, much of it involving prominent figures. Published versions remain, often with no proof offered or asked.

There was talk of the Abolitionist leader, Thaddeus Stevens, and his handsome quadroon housekeeper, Lydia Smith, or "Mrs. Stevens," the widow of a Negro barber from Gettysburg—a case in which an investigator finds no supporting documents.

Charges followed Generals Judson Kilpatrick and George Custer through several theaters of war, and some of them crept into documentary form. It was only after World War II that the file on "Annie Jones" was made public, a case involving both these Federal generals.

The National Archives now counts among its treasures a confession of Annie Jones, a native of Cambridge, Massachusetts, who was eighteen when the war broke out. She openly testified that she was a prostitute following the Union Army in Virginia, and that her services were in brisk demand.

As early as 1879 one John Labine of Boston asked the War Department for a copy of this file, and was told by the office of the Adjutant General: "It is not deemed advisable or conducive to the public interest to furnish the copies requested."

Among Annie Jones's admissions in the Archives are these:

> While in the various camps I was furnished by the commanding officers with a tent and sometimes occupied quarters with the officers. . . . In the fall of 1862 I went to the Army of the Potomac. . . . General Kilpatrick became very jealous because of General Custer's attentions to me and went to General Meade's headquarters and charged me with being a Rebel spy. . . .
>
> I spent two and a half years in the Union army. . . . I invariably wore a major's straps. . . . I was employed as a private friend or companion. . . . I have led a very roving, and, it may be, questionable, life.

Annie was put into Old Capitol Prison, and became a sensation even there. Because of alleged intimacies with her, a guard from Massachusetts was dismissed, and details of the case were bandied in the press.

General Custer denied illicit relations with Annie and swore that, though she had visited his camp twice, she had not lodged in his tent. He said flatly, "Her statement in relation to Gen. Kilpatrick and myself is simply untrue." Kilpatrick had nothing to say. The investigation came to an end.

Other, more celebrated, cases were not lacking in documentation. A Union soldier newspaper published in Beaufort, South Carolina, in June, 1863, gave the troops details of the divorce obtained by their commander, General John M. Brannan, once Sherman's chief of artillery.

The paper traced the lively career of Mrs. Brannan, nee Eliza Crane, who ran away with the socially prominent Powell T. Wyman, an army officer who was killed during the war.

The decision of the court reflected the temper of the times in such cases:

> The wife, under one of those strange and wicked caprices that set at defiance the vows of marriage and the obligations of honor, of respectable parentage and respectable kindred, broke loose from her marriage relations, and took up her abode with a Mr. Powell T. Wyman . . .

While Brannon advertised for her in the United States, and had lakes dragged for her body, fearing that she had met with foul play, she lived in Italy with Wyman. Brannan did not cease his search.

The decision commented:

> During all this time, it appears, she was cooly speculating in prostitution on the other side of the Atlantic. . . . I look upon this as one of the most aggravated and one of the most cruel instances of infidelity upon record, and do not hesitate to decree a divorce to General Brannan with the restoration to him of all the rights of an unmarried man and the custody of the only offspring of this marriage.

The most sensational mixture of divorce and alleged romance during the war was the case of General Earl Van Dorn, a dashing Confederate officer murdered in Spring Hill, Tennessee by Dr. George B. Peters.

Peters divorced his young and charming wife about the

time of Van Dorn's shooting, but they were later reunited. There is one tradition that the general was shot because of a quarrel over business matters, but a stronger one involves romance.

In the Jefferson Davis papers of the Duke University library is a letter of May 11, 1863, a report from General P.B. Starke to Jefferson Davis on Van Dorn's death, written shortly after the murder.

Starke wrote:

> Since my telegram to you I have taken some pains to ascertain what were the particulars in regard to the shooting of General Van Dorn by Dr. Peters and have but little to add.
>
> After conversing with one of the late General's staff officers I find that Dr. Peters was induced to kill the General in consequence of his familiarity with Mrs. Peters in visiting her and remaining at her house until late hours of the night—and that in the absence of the Doctor.
>
> The impropriety of his conduct was freely discussed and condemned in and out of the army. That he was a gallant soldier and pure patriot is conceded by all. The only question discussed is as to the manner in which he was killed. The Doctor went into his room and found him alone. The firing of a pistol caused his staff to go into the room. They met the Doctor coming out, who mounted his horse and rode rapidly off.
>
> I did not see the body, but it is stated by his friends that he was shot in the back of the head and it is supposed that the General was sitting at his table when the Doctor shot him from behind.
>
> That the General had great weaknesses in such matters must be admitted.

There are frequent further glimpses into the private lives of the leading characters of Civil War literature, most of them only glimpses.

In March, 1865, as Sherman's army poured through North Carolina in the final phases of action, cavalry commanded by the boy major general, Judson Kilpatrick, was surprised in a dawn attack on the present site of Fort Bragg. As General Joe Wheeler's horsemen scattered the Federal invaders, Kilpatrick dashed for safety clad in his underwear; he escaped by directing a Confederate rider toward a figure disappearing in a swamp. "There goes the General!"

The Confederate version of the incident: Kilpatrick was interrupted in an intimate scene with a woman camp follower.

The Federal version: The General had gone out in shirt and underwear, as was his custom, to see to his horses at dawn.

One item of agreement: A number of women accompanied the Federal cavalry headquarters, most of them refugees who had traveled with Kilpatrick the long route from Savannah, Georgia.

Even so impressive a figure as the Confederate teetotaler Jeb Stuart did not escape the gossips. One woman, who signed herself only "Southern Lady," wrote to Jefferson Davis from Culpeper, Virginia:

> If General Stuart is allowed to remain our commanding general of cavalry we are lost people. I have been eye witness to the maneuvering of General Stuart since he has been in Culpeper. . . . Gen. S. loves the admiration of his class of lady friends too much to be a commanding general. He loves to have his repeated reviews immediately under the Yankees' eyes too much for the benefit and pleasure of his lady friends for the interest of the Confederacy.

Stuart's friends on the President's staff passed the letter to Jeb with a playful admonition that he "cease your attentions to the ladies or make them more general."

Stuart was moved to tell his wife's cousin, John Esten Cooke, "That person does not live who can say that I ever did anything improper of that description."

Stuart's aide, Captain William Blackford, was also vigorous in his defense of his chief's innocence—and in the process laid claim to a certain Argus-eyed omniscience:

> Though he dearly loved to kiss a pretty girl, and the pretty girls loved to kiss him, he was as pure as they. . . .

I know this to be true, for it would have been impossible
for it to have been otherwise and I not to have known it.

Numerous incidents involving sex and kindred matters
were reported during the sack of Columbia, South Carolina, by
troops of Sherman. One witness, Dr. D.H. Trezevant, who had
much to say of acts of violence in the city, reported on sights in
the streets:

> It was not unusual to see a Yankee soldier with his arm
> around the neck of a negro wench, even in the common
> thoroughfare, or hugging and kissing a mulatto girl, when
> he could find one so degraded that she would not spurn him
> for his impudence and want of common decency.

27

The Submarine Hunley

IN the chill dusk of February 17, 1864, as the moon rose over Charleston harbor, history's first successful submarine attack got under way.

Out from the besieged Confederate city came a singular craft, the 25-foot *H.L. Hunley*, a converted boiler tank bearing a torpedo at her bow and a crew of eight volunteers inside. Six of these men were cranking at her propellor to reach a speed of four miles an hour. An infantry lieutenant steered her, a compass and crude depth gauge at his side. Now and then he peered through the glass of a hatch.

The little submarine lumbered along just under the surface, borne by the dying outward tide through Breach Inlet, between Sullivan's Island and the Isle of Palms. At the mouth of the harbor lay the Federal blockading fleet: an inner ring of iron-clads protected by nets of chains, and beyond, a fleet of wooden ships, the *Hunley*'s game tonight.

The sub bore no Confederate device, for she was owned by private parties, built for the profitable business of sinking enemy vessels as prizes. Her builders, at any rate, had a letter of marque for underwater privateering from a New Orleans collector of customs dated 1862. But several of her owners and builders, including the man for whom she was named, had perished in their experimental boat.

It is now uncertain whether the little vessel stalked prizes for her crew this night, or mere glory for the Confederacy. She sailed, however, under orders from General P.G.T. Beauregard, commander of Charleston's defenses.

Her skipper was Lieutenant George E. Dixon, late of Company E, 21st Alabama Volunteers. In his crew were C.F. Carlson of the Wagner Artillery, Arnold Becker, James A. Wicks, C. Simkins, F. Collins, one Ridgeway of the Confederate Navy, and a man named Miller.

Dixon shied away from the ironclads of the first line and approached the wooden ships. He knew that he might be seen at close quarters in the moonlight, but there was no help for it. The *Hunley* was so feeble that she could not fight her way back to shore unless an incoming tide favored her.

The ungainly craft came at last—near 8:45 P.M.—alongside an enemy warship. This was the steam sloop *Housatonic*, of 1,240 tons, not quite two years old, armed with thirteen guns. Dixon bore in on her, unaware that he had been seen from above. The historic attack was at hand.

Behind the little submersible was a long story of death by drowning and suffocation, and of persistence almost as grim. The first model, built in New Orleans in 1861, was a 19-foot porpoiselike tub known as the *Pioneer*, made of heavy iron plates, its chief distinction a crude "snorkel" for breathing fresh air, fashioned from a tube and float. Its owners were two marine engineers, Baxter Watson and James R. McClintock, and a businessman, Robert R. Barrow, who counted among his assets a wealthy brother-in-law, Horace Lawson Hunley.

The financial backer of the project, Hunley was a native of Sumner County, Tennessee, thirty-six years old as war came. He had spent most of his life in New Orleans. These were patriots, but the spur was profit, and when the *Pioneer* made a successful dive in Lake Ponchartrain and blew up a barge with a torpedo, its backers were elated. A later test brought death to a crew of four, but on March 31 the group got a privateers' "license"—a letter of marque—to attack Federal shipping.

A surprise Federal assault ended this phase, and the day before Admiral David Farragut took the city, on April 27, 1862, the *Pioneer* was sunk in Ponchartrain to save her from the enemy. It was not until 1878 that a boy swimmer found her and she was raised to lie rusting as a lakeside exhibit for a generation. She now belongs to the Louisiana State Museum, and is in the arcade of the *Presbytère* in New Orleans.

The builders fled to Mobile (just half an hour's drive from today's nuclear sub pens at Pascagoula, Mississippi). There they found a machine shop, Parks and Lyons, and a seasoned British machinist, William A. Alexander, who had been in this country only three years. McClintock and Watson furnished the design, Hunley the money, and Alexander the builder's skill. A new model was soon complete, but sank in her first trials at Fort Morgan, without loss of life. Now began the *H.L. Hunley*.

An old boiler, 25 feet long, was cut in half lengthwise, a tapered bow and stern added, and crude ballast tanks were made just under the skin. Heavy iron strips were bolted to the bottom as ballast, so that they could be dropped from within by turning the bolts, to lighten the ship. Hand pumps were devised to empty the ballast tanks, which could be filled simply by opening sea cocks.

Two hatches rose from the top, no more than eight inches high, with glass plates in top and side, sealed with rubber gaskets. There was an air box above, too, fitted with a shaft so that fresh air could be admitted at will—provided the ship lay quite near the surface.

An iron shaft was run through the sub, bent to form handles by which eight crew members could turn it like a crank. A propeller, shielded by an iron ring, was attached before the rudder. The killing weapon was a torpedo, designed to be towed on a 200-foot rope and smashed against enemy hulls by the diving tank.

The boat exploded a flatboat target on her first run, but had trouble in the rough waters of Mobile Bay; whether she lost her first crew there is uncertain, but in late summer she was sent to Charleston by rail, to help General Beauregard loosen the blockade of that city. She got a new crew on the South Carolina coast, led by Lieutenant John Payne, a volunteer Alabama army officer.

To her builder, Alexander, the boat was simplicity itself in operation: When all hands were aboard and the hatches fastened, a candle was lighted by the skipper and water let into the tanks until the sub lay three inches under water. The cocks closed, the boat got under way with the crewmen laboring at their cranks. The captain had only to lower a lever to depress his diving fins, taking the boat to a desired level; the *Hunley* would remain at that depth until he turned the fins upward—in theory.

One night the sub lay at her Charleston wharf, the crew below in their places, wedged so tightly that no one could pass fore or aft. Lieutenant Payne stood forward, ready to pull down the hatch, when the wake of a passing steamer washed over the deck, swamping the *Hunley* and sending her to the bottom. Payne wriggled out of the open hatch, but was the only survivor.

Beauregard was persuaded to approve another test after the success of a kindred craft, a surface torpedo boat, the tiny *David*. This midget had damaged the menacing Federal monitor *New Ironsides* with explosives, and despite the capture of her captain and a hail of rifle fire, was saved by two of her crew.

The *Hunley*'s troubles were not soon over. In another trial she lost a second crew of volunteers, with Lieutenant Payne and two others crawling from a hatch to safety. Beauregard's waning faith in the boat was revived by the arrival of Horace Hunley himself, who begged to be allowed to try again. One diving test was successful, but on October 15, 1863, Hunley went down to his death with a fresh crew.

Now Dixon and Alexander came from Mobile, but Beauregard would not consent to a new trial until the craft had been raised and examined. The general watched as the sub was opened:

"The unfortunate men were contorted into all kinds of horrible attitudes; some clutching candles, evidently endeavoring to force open the manholes; others lying in the bottom tightly grappled together, and the blackened faces of all presented the expression of their despair and agony."

Even this was overcome by Dixon and Alexander, who urged another trial—and by a staff officer, who suggested that the *Hunley* be operated as a surface vessel, like the *David*, carrying her torpedo on a spar at the bow. Beauregard relented.

The determined experts looked beyond the death agonies of the victims: The *Hunley* had lain with her bow deep in mud, at 35 degrees. The bolts of the hatches had not been removed; Hunley was forward, his right hand over his head, as if trying to raise the hatch against heavy pressure. An unlighted candle was in his left hand and the sea cock was open. Dixon and Alexander reasoned that Hunley had opened the cock, then tried to light his candle and to drop the iron ballast from the bottom, working feverishly as the sub slipped downward. Hunley seemed to have forgotten that he had not closed the sea cock, and to have finally exhausted himself at the hand pump.

Dixon and Alexander, convinced of the seaworthiness of their boat, soon put her into condition. They got a volunteer crew from the Navy's receiving ship, *Indian Chief*—though Beauregard insisted that they tell every man the gruesome history of the craft before signing him on.

Weeks of intensive practice began. The crew walked seven miles from barracks to the boat daily, and drove her in the waters of Back Bay. Dixon and Alexander took a daily fix on the nearest Federal blockade ship by lying flat on the sands and sighting across a compass—and by night they tried to steer for the targets. Bad weather prevented an attack, but the outings proved useful as experience.

The winds were contrary from November into February, and there was no chance to slip from the harbor to strike at the outer ships. Part of the time was spent in tinkering with the faulty air supply of the vessel, which proved insufficient through the wooden chute of the air box. The final test was a near thing.

Determined to see how long she could remain submerged, Dixon and Alexander loaded their crew late one day, as a crowd of soldiers watched from shore. The crew agreed that the first man to find himself at the end of his endurance should yell "Up!" and the officers would take them to the surface.

The *Hunley* went down smoothly, a single candle lit within. After twenty-five minutes by Alexander's watch the candle guttered out for lack of oxygen and the men sat in darkness in the tube at the bottom of the bay. Darkness had fallen overhead, too, and watchers dispersed. A messenger to Beauregard reported that still another crew had been lost in the experimental coffin. Below, the nine men waited.

At last, as Alexander remembered it, every man gasped "Up!" in a single voice, and the officers began working the pumps. The boat pitched steeply underfoot as the bow rose, for the stern was held fast to the bottom. Alexander knew that something had fouled his pump, and he calmly removed the cap, lifted out a valve, and as sea water rushed in, pulled seaweed through the opening and replaced the parts.

Some of the crew "almost lost control of themselves," but the stern rose as the ballast was pumped out, and the hatches at last flew open over the gasping men who were so near to asphyxiation. They could see but a single man ashore, a soldier who did not sight them until Alexander called, and then the soldier tossed him a line. Alexander looked at his watch by candlelight. They had been down two hours and thirty-five minutes.

Men at Beauregard's headquarters hailed the unexpected crew the next morning, but some staff officers scoffed at the claim that the sub had lain below for so long. There was no longer a question about the attack, however. Everyone agreed that the *Hunley* was ready.

As the time neared Alexander was recalled to Mobile to work on a repeating cannon then under development, and despite his protests, missed the fiery debut of his little boat.

The Federal fleet was aware that some strange Rebel craft might attack; others had come down from Admiral John Dahlgren with a warning, based on rumors and intelligence reports.

Even so, Acting Master J.K. Crosby was astonished when

he looked down from the deck of the *Housatonic* just before nine o'clock.

Crosby was officer of the deck for the night, and his sharp eye detected something huge and dark in the water about a hundred yards off. The night was calm, with a light sea running. There was no wind, and the moon was becoming brighter by the moment. A slight mist lay on the water, but it was so thin that visibility was good as far as the neighboring ships of the fleet. The usual lookouts were posted on the forecastle, the gangway, and quarterdeck. From the latter post Crosby saw the object, and thought it must be a porpoise. The ship's quartermaster was nearby, and after looking through his glass said that the dark mystery was a school of fish. As the object came on toward the ship Crosby sounded the alarm, ordered a beat to quarters, slipped the anchor chain, and called the captain.

Officers and men poured on deck. The apparition was quite close by now, a dark body moving slowly, trailing phosphorescent light. The captain ordered cannon fired at it, but the guns could not be depressed far enough. Several men shot rifles and muskets without obvious effect, and the captain blazed at the sub with a shotgun.

The *Housatonic*, no longer at anchor, began to drift by the stern; her engines began turning. The sub was now nearing the ship's hull, and the engines drove the two together. There was a tremendous explosion. Timbers and splinters were flung high into the air, and Crosby thought that the stern had been blown off. There was a "fearful rushing of water" and heavy black smoke rolled from the stack. The *Housatonic* began to settle.

There were already casualties, but the men were not struck by panic, and got the port lifeboats into position. Just as they did so a lurch of the ship swamped the boats on that side. The starboard boats were soon lowered and the men and officers who had leaped into the water were rescued. The captain, who had been flung into the air by the explosion, was unhurt, and soon led his crew to the nearby USS *Canandaigua* in one of the boats. By muster time next morning, only five crewmen were missing.

The *Housatonic* had gone down in about twenty-eight feet of water, her fatal wound on the starboard side near the mizzenmast. Crosby saw a ten-foot square blown out of her quarterdeck, with the heavy spanker boom snapped in its thickest part. The water for some distance was white with splinters of wood. Within four minutes after the explosion, the *Housatonic* had sunk.

Confederates ashore knew nothing of the successful attack and only when a small enemy boat was captured later in the year did they learn of the *Housatonic*'s fate. Even the Federals knew little, except that the sloop had sunk like a stone. A hastily summoned court of inquiry concluded that some kind of torpedo boat had been at work. Confederate experts decided that the *Hunley* had been lost, had probably driven into the gaping hole in her victim's hull, and dragged her crew to their deaths.

Exactly a year after the attack, enjoying a respite due chiefly to *Hunley*-inspired fears, Charleston's weakened defenses fell. After the war Federal divers found the wounded *Houstaonic* and moved her to clear North Channel. A buoy was placed to mark her new location, and she was later blown up.

When the sloop was moved the first time, divers reported seeing the *Hunley* lying nearby, and one of them said he touched her propeller. She was not moved, however, and though her location is known, she has evaded modern divers and still rests on the bottom of Charleston Harbor—by fifty years the first successful submarine, and until World War II the only American sub to sink an enemy vessel.

28

Lincoln's Subs

ABRAHAM LINCOLN narrowly missed becoming the father of modern undersea warfare; the President encountered a submariner almost two and a half years before the *Hunley* made history.

The inventor was a striking figure, Brutus de Villeroi, who had come from France to offer a 35-foot screw-driven sub which was now at the Philadelphia Navy Yard. Lincoln was fascinated by the details, for de Villeroi was no tyro. As long ago as 1835, in his home town of Nantes, he had submerged in a 10-foot submarine for two hours—probably enchanting a seven-year-old fellow townsman, Jules Verne.

The craft offered by de Villeroi in September, 1861, had a secret chemical device to provide fresh air, the inventor said. It could remain under water for three hours without danger to its crew.

At Lincoln's insistence the Navy tested the sub, was impressed, and ordered a larger model built. The first Federal submarine, the *Alligator*, was the result, but it was crippled by a squabble between de Villeroi and the contractor over the breathing apparatus and its mean of propulsion. The Frenchman left in disgust and dropped out of the war.

His *Alligator*, minus its fresh-air machine and driven by a bank of oars rather than a propeller, invaded Hampton Roads in June, 1862, but did no more than poke about on the bottom. It was soon lost while under tow at sea—foundering in the same rough waters off Cape Hatteras, North Carolina, which were the grave of the *Monitor*.

Even so Lincoln was not through. In the week of the *Monitor-Merrimac* duel the President tried to interest the Navy in a rocket-driven submarine offered by Pascal Plant, a Washington inventor; experts brushed it aside as a daydream.

Plant was soon back with a lesser weapon: the world's first rocket-driven torpedo. In a test at the Washington Navy Yard witnessed by Secretary of Navy Gideon Welles the pioneer weapon was fired in December, 1862.

One torpedo blew up a mudbank, and a second veered crazily from course to sink the *Diana*, a little schooner anchored nearby. This was the first driven torpedo to sink a ship, but it seemed to critical officers to hold little promise.

A month later the rocket-driven tube finally snapped the patience of the Navy when, under test, one of Plant's torpedoes leaped from the water of the Anacostia River some twenty feet from its launching site, soared into the air and splashed back into the river a full hundred yards away. The significance of the flying missile was lost on observers, who disbanded in disgust.

29

What They Said About
U.S. Grant

NO major figure of the war attracted more gossip than General Grant, whose talents were long hidden by his modest, self-effacing manner. In his swift wartime rise, whispers about him became campaigns of slander in newspapers, letters and government reports. Washington sent more than one spy to report on Grant in the field.

Some of the more spectacular charges:

Charge: *Grant was a slave-owner who had voted the Democratic ticket and married into a pro-Southern family.*
True.

In 1858 Grant bought a mulatto, William Jones, thirty-five, but gave him freedom after a year, though desperately in need of money the slave would have brought.

He voted for the Democrat, Buchanan, he said, hoping that the Union could be held together by compromise.

Grant married Julia Dent of St. Louis, who owned at least three slaves; her family was pro-Southern. Grant differed sharply with his father-in law on slavery, and before the war returned his wife's slaves to her family.

Charge: *Grant was offered command of the Confederate armies, and was persuaded not to accept by Stephen A. Douglas.*
Branded as false by historians, this is a persistent tradition in the Douglas family. No documents support the claim, and despite

a meeting of Grant and Douglas in Springfield, Illinois, in the spring of 1861, when Grant was depressed over delay in winning a Federal commission, the story has an unlikely sound.

Charge: *Grant sired a half-breed daughter by an Indian woman at a Vancouver army post.*

Apparently false. When these whispers were heard during the war, an Army wife who had lived at Vancouver branded them as "baseless and malicious," and recalled the truth—that a man named Richard Grant lived with a squaw at a nearby post and had several half-breed children.

Charge: *Grant was a drunkard as a young officer in Western posts, and was ousted from the army as a result.*

A half-truth, or exaggeration. Grant had a problem with alcohol, but none of the many witnesses who knew him in the West pictured him as a drunkard.

Lieutenant Henry Hodges, who knew Grant at Vancouver, said that he went on "two or three sprees a year," but that when scolded by friends he promised to stop drinking, and did so.

A contractor at Fort Humboldt, California, said, "Grant took to liquor, not by any means in enormous quantities . . . he had a poor brain for drinking . . . in all other respects he was a man of unusual self-control and thoroughly the master of his appetites."

Captain Grenville Haller, of Fort Humboldt, said Grant was a four-finger drinker, who drank that amount in a tumbler, often several times daily.

Grant resigned from the army in April, 1854, without warning. An officer who interviewed several of Grant's friends reported that Grant was tipsy when on duty at his paymaster's table, and that his unfriendly commander, Colonel Robert Buchanan, asked him to resign or face charges.

The process of resignation was touched with irony. Grant's letter was addressed to Colonel Samuel Cooper, the U.S. Adjutant General, who would soon serve the Confederacy in that capacity. His resignation was accepted by the Secretary of War, Jefferson Davis.

Charge: *Grant was drunk at the battle of Shiloh, causing surprise and near-annihilation of his army.*

Certainly false. Numerous diarists and witnesses, some of them outside Grant's immediate circle, testified as to Grant's sobriety at this time. His sponsor, Congressman Elihu Washburne of Illinois, was moved to say on the floor of the House: "There is no more temperate man in the army than General Grant. He never indulges in the use of intoxicating liquors at all."

This did not quiet critics, but the Army and official Washington was content. General Henry Halleck, by no means a Grant partisan, reported that the army was not surprised at Shiloh. At least no Federal soldiers were killed in bed, as early reports had it; Grant probably made serious miscalculations as to the numbers and proximity of the Confederates in front, but his troops actually opened the battle with attack.

Charge: *Grant went on a spree in the days just before the surrender of Vicksburg.*

A matter of controversy. A Chicago *Times* reporter, Sylvanus Cadwallader, left a persuasive account of finding Grant drunk on a steamboat, locking him in a stateroom to keep him away from liquor—and flinging bottles from a porthole into the river, all over Grant's vehement protests. The story, however, was written some thirty years later.

Of this episode, Charles A. Dana, a War Department observer, said only that Grant was ill and abed. A day or so later Grant's most intimate friend in the army, General John A. Rawlins, wrote his superior: "The great solicitude which I feel for the safety of this army leads me to mention what I hoped never again to do—the subject of your drinking."

Some modern scholars still question Cadwallader's story.

Charge: *Grant permitted profiteers, including his father, to speculate in cotton within his lines.*

False. Grant's father went into partnership with Simon, Henry, and Harmon Mack—Mack and Brothers, a firm of Jewish merchants—apparently offering them General Grant's protection for their trading operations in the field, without advising his son. When the Macks made their proposal to Grant, he angrily shipped them home.

This case led to another stigma on Grant's reputation.

Charge: *Grant was anti-Semitic.*

There is some doubt as to the circumstances and even authorship, but at least the controversial General Order Number 11 went out over Grant's name:

> The Jews, as a class violating every regulation of trade established by the Treasury Department and also department orders, are hereby expelled from the department within twenty-four hours from the receipt of this order.

> Post commanders will see that all of this class of people be furnished passes and required to leave, and any one returning . . . will be arrested and held in confinement until an opportunity occurs of sending them out as prisoners.

Washington overruled Grant almost immediately, and he willingly withdrew the order, but the damage was done.

Charge: *Grant was anti-Catholic.*

There seems to be little or no basis for this attack, which arose from the case of Father Paul Gillen, a well-known Irish-born priest who served widely in the armies. Gillen traveled in a rockaway with his folding altar and chapel tent, holding services throughout Grant's department. The general ousted him under an order forbidding "citizens" in the military area, and reportedly put him under arrest. Gillen joined the 170th New York as chaplain, and ended the affair.

Charge: *Grant held personal grudges against some who had bested him in civilian life, and took revenge in the army.*

A flimsy charge, based on Grant's futile race for the $1,500-a-year post of County Surveyor for St. Louis County, Illinois, in 1859. A German, Eberhard Salomon, defeated him, leading Grant to bitter comments on foreigners in public office.

During the war, Grant was charged with deliberately with-holding a report on the victory of General Freiderich Salomon, brother to Eberhard, in a battle at Fort Helena, Arkansas.

The familiar story that President Lincoln, told of Grant's drinking habits, wished for some of that brand of whiskey for his other generals, is apochryphal. The story traces back to ancient history, and has been told of several kings and their generals.

What the Union soldiers in ranks thought of this oft-slandered commander was summed up by one of his privates: "Everything that Grant directs is right. His soldiers believe in him. . . . I have never heard a single soldier speak in doubt of Grant."

30

Dixie

THE name "Dixie" is probably a bit of Franco-American slang born in the Mississippi river-boat trade, though some say it derived from the Mason-Dixon line, the surveyor's boundary between Pennsylvania and Maryland. It had become a universal nickname for the South long before the war; it seems to have had its origin in that most endearing of commodities, money.

Unlike many Southern banks, the prospering Creole financial houses of New Orleans dealt at par; their notes were traded at face value, and no deductions were made or asked in the brisk trade which came downriver into the gay Louisiana city.

The most popular of these bank notes was a ten-dollar bill. Its French heritage was clear in the cheery legend on each corner: "Dix." To unlettered tradesmen, stevedores and boatmen, these bills were only "Dixies," and as their soundness became known in the great river basin, the lower South became "Dixieland," and the term was familiar on the exotic landscape of the waterway and its commerce.

It was 1859 before the word made its formal debut in song —though the embryonic Southern anthem or something quite like it had been sung on plantations and steamer decks for generations. Its recorded birth, however, was in New York, on a rainy April Sunday of '59. The author was Daniel Decatur Emmett, a forty-four-year-old Ohio boy who had run away from home, served as an army fifer, played with circus bands and worked with minstrel shows.

When he was still sixteen, Emmett turned out a hit song of the times, "Old Dan Tucker," and thus, when Dan Bryant of Bryant's Minstrels called for a lively new "walkaround" song to be played in New York streets as a lure for his '59 show, Emmett was his man.

The song was an overnight sensation, and was sung literally everywhere in the country. Many companies pirated the tune and parodied the words, and from such a case in New Orleans the song swept the South.

Years later, when the Confederacy had adopted the song, Emmett said he rued the day it was written, since it had become a hallmark of treason. He also confessed that the tune did not spring full-blown into his head. The opening, he said, came from an old song his mother had crooned to him as a babe in arms, a rather wicked little ditty which began, "Come, Philander, let's be marchin'."

The minstrel-show tune was only that until February 18, 1861, when Jefferson Davis was inducted into office as President of the Confederacy in Montgomery, Alabama. A little procession wound toward the hilltop capitol behind a band directed by Herman Arnold, a naturalized German music teacher of the town.

Arnold had hastily orchestrated the number for his men, under the title "I Wish I Was in Dixie's Land"—and under the impression that he had originated the piece himself from the raw material of folklore.

As the tune provoked its first public foot-tappings to parade time, Davis and Vice-President Alexander Stephens rolled along in a borrowed carriage, elaborately hung with silk and upholstered in yellow and white, drawn by spotless white horses. Soldiers of the 1st Alabama were the escort, the first men to march to the peppy measures.

Abraham Lincoln also liked the song. Just a little more than four years after its Montgomery debut, when he was in the last week of his life, Lincoln took "Dixie" back into the Union. It was April 8, 1865, just at dusk, when Lincoln had returned from a tour of his army camps below fallen Richmond. He was worn but happy as he settled on the paddle-wheel steamer *River Queen* in harbor where the James met the Appomattox. To the west, Grant was closing in on Lee, and the President was ready to return to Washington.

A Federal Army band came aboard and began a serenade. After a few numbers, including the "Marseillaise," Lincoln turned to a guest, a young French count: "Have you heard the Rebel song, 'Dixie'?"

The count shook his head.

"The tune is now Federal property," Lincoln said, "and it's good to show the Rebels that with us in power, they will be free to hear it again. It has always been a favorite of mine, and since we've captured it, we have a perfect right to enjoy it."

The musicians seemed surprised when the President called for the tune, but they blared away, the music carrying over the water to the army camps. In the audience on board was a mulatto seamstress, Elizabeth Keckley, a servant to Mrs. Lincoln. Before the war she had served another woman high in Washington society, Mrs. Jefferson Davis.

Whatever her thoughts as she heard the symbolic tune, Elizabeth recorded only: "The band at once struck up 'Dixie,' that sweet, inspiriting air; and when the music died away there was clapping of hands and other applause."

Within a few minutes the *River Queen* slipped away downstream, bearing Lincoln on the last trip of his life.

31

Symbols of the Lost Cause

ON a Richmond Street one day, so the story goes, a drunken
Confederate soldier met Jefferson Davis, and stared, thunder-
struck.

"Are you Mister Davis?"

"I am."

"Ain't you President of the Confederate States?"

"I am, sir."

"Well, by God, I thought you looked like a postage stamp."

This was by no means the final tribute to the storied postal
system of the Confederacy. Today's heirs of this soldier's well-
tempered awe might include the thousand-odd members of the
Confederate Stamp Alliance, a nationwide skein of experts pre-
siding over one of the most complex fields of philately.

In a 1956 stamp auction a group of "provisional" Confederate stamps and covers from one collection sold for over $234,-
000—and the peak was for one envelope bearing two stamps
issued at Livingston, Alabama, bought by a dealer for $14,000,
and quickly resold. Many Confederate stamps and covers have
sold for more than $1,000 each.

This empire of hobbyists was not built by rarity alone, for
the Confederate postal system has been colorful from the start.
The Southern Post Office was the only department of either
warring government to show a profit in the conflict. It was
bidden to do so by law, and driven to it by Postmaster General
John H. Reagan, who later became godfather to our Interstate
Commerce Commission. Profits were achieved by doubling, then

redoubling postal rates, by using United States stamps with Federal approval during the first months, by eliminating franked mail even for Congressmen, using stamps for fractional currency, making sharp deals with railroads and allowing draft immunity to mail contractors.

Reagan was the third choice of the Confederacy for this post, but turned out to be the only permanent member of the Cabinet. The outbreak of war at Fort Sumter deprived Reagen of the finer Northern-made stamps he sought, and he accepted lithographed substitutes made in Richmond by the firm of Ludwig & Hoyer, which used stone plates, rather than copper or steel. Charles Hoyer designed these stamps, drawing them free-hand, thereby adding interest for today's collectors.

A sample of Hoyer's work is the ten-cent stamp showing a head of Thomas Jefferson. The letter "A" in "CSA" is un-crossed—and though Jefferson, a passable likeness, was copied from a United States stamp, his left ear is missing.

Another work by Hoyer was a stone engraving of Jefferson Davis from a *carte de visite* photograph, a striking likeness which adorned the only American postal stamp to portray a living man.

Before these stamps appeared Confederate postmasters made free use of United States stocks on hand, and after June 1, 1861, when both sides agreed to end this period, postmasters made their own stamps. These were lithographs, typed stamps, or woodcuts, producing a variety of the rare "handstamped paids" and "provisionals" for collectors.

The prewar rate for half-ounce letters was three cents; the Confederacy boosted it to five cents, with a 500-mile delivery zone, and ten cents beyond. In July, 1862, the base rate went to ten cents, and the Post Office became self-sustaining.

One of the chief mysteries of the wartime mail service was the smuggling of a crew of experts from a New York banknote firm into Richmond, where they formed a new company and made the first Confederate copperplate stamps. The company was Archer & Daly, its chief John Archer, a skilled engraver from the North; his partner was Joseph Daly, a Richmond plasterer and politician.

Archer & Daly figured in the classic stamp story of the Confederacy:

Frederick Volck, a foreign sculptor who lived in Richmond, covertly made a bust of Jefferson Davis by attending church each Sunday for weeks, sitting near the President, studying his head without attracting attention.

When the completed bust was unveiled, Richmond society greeted it with delight; it won a place of honor in the Confederate White House, and was chosen as the design for another stamp. A proof of the stamp was approved by the President and by Colonel H. St. George Offutt, chief of the contracting bureau —but there was trouble ahead.

An eccentric Englishman who seemed to wield a social tyranny over the Davis household, Colonel W.H. Browne, was wounded because he had not been consulted in this artistic project. Browne was an aide to Davis, and during a reception at the Mansion he approached Mrs. Davis:

"Have you seen the new stamp they have made of the President?"

"No. Could I see it?"

Browne took from his pocket a sample proof, and with one breath doomed the stamp:

"Note the strong resemblance to President Lincoln."

The stamp was withdrawn from circulation almost immediately without fanfare. The result was a relatively rare stamp, and one hailed by collectors as perhaps the finest produced in the South, dominated by a simple drawing of the head of Davis with a cameolike quality.

Among other stamp lore:

The Richmond jeweler, J.T. Paterson, who migrated to Columbia, South Carolina, and then to Augusta, Georgia, with a crew of experts produced stamps and money for the Confederacy by lithography. Until recent years he was unknown to collectors.

The Archer & Daly firm disappeared late in the war as Grant enclosed Richmond with his armies, and its plates reappeared in Columbia, South Carolina, where the firm of Keatinge & Ball printed stamps until Sherman sacked that city.

The only foreign-printed stamps used in America were produced during the war, smuggled through the blockade from England. The house of Thos. de la Rue & Co. shipped more than 5,000,000 stamps on the blockade-runner *Bermuda*, which was captured, and her cargo sold at public auction. The stamps were tossed overboard by her anxious skipper, but a small packet survived, to appear in collections.

The shipment was replaced by a hasty order for 12,000,000 more five-cent stamps and a set of plates, and these arrived safely.

Confederate Money

Southern presses (at first aided by the National Bank Note Company of New York) ground out more than two billion dollars' worth of currency during the war—and this was perhaps matched by the endless issues of states, counties, cities, railroads, merchants, and business houses of all kinds. Counterfeits and "souvenir bills" added to the storm.

A feature of the last formal meeting of the Confederate Cabinet on March 18, 1865, was a veto of the Eighth Issue of

Confederate currency to the tune of eighty million dollars. President Davis said that approval of the issue "would be accepted as a proof that there is no limit to the issue of Treasury notes."

When Confederate "blue backs" appeared in 1861, they were valued at ninety-five cents on the dollar, in gold, and though they were never accepted as legal tender, their theoretical backing with Southern cotton gave them temporarily high standing.

These bank notes began life with a promise that within a year they would be redeemed, with interest of a cent per day on each hundred dollars. A following issue offered payment within two years after a treaty of peace with the North—and a third, just after the victory at First Manassas, or Bull Run, cut this time to six months. Interest also rose later, to two cents daily.

The rapid deterioration of Confederate money provided a classic pattern for inflation in a nation waging an unsuccessful war.

By 1863 the notes were worth thirty-three cents on the dollar. By the time of Appomattox, the value was 1.6 cents to the dollar. On May 1, 1865, the last known date of active trading, these notes were handled in bales—1,200 for one dollar.

(The Federal Government, driven to issue paper money for the first time since days of the Revolution with its "greenbacks" originating in 1861, had brief difficulties, but the low point of the greenback's value was thirty-nine cents on the dollar in July, 1864.)

The first notes of the Confederacy were called The Montgomery Issue, after the first capital of the new nation, and were printed in New York and smuggled South. These denominations were $50, $100, $500 and $1,000. In 1960, several sets of these bills, one of each included, had sold to collectors for more than $2,000.

From the start Southern financiers and engravers placed patriotism second, and used Yankee scenes and figures on their bills. The first $500 note featured a farm landscape with cattle and a train crossing (complete even as to the railroad sign: "Look out for bell rings.") The design was stolen from a one-dollar note issued by the North Western Bank of Warren, Pennsylvania.

Other designs, like Negroes picking cotton, came from Southern life; from classic mythology; and from American history (John Calhoun, Andrew Jackson, George Washington, American Indians). Later designs ran strongly to Confederate officials and heroes: Judah P. Benjamin, C.G. Memminger, R.M.T. Hunter, Vice-President Alexander Stephens, Jefferson Davis, George Randolph, Stonewall Jackson, Senator Clement C. Clay, and Mrs. Lucy Pickens, wife of a Governor of South Carolina.

One amusing design was that of a ten-dollar bill copied from a prewar note of the Mechanics Savings Bank of Savannah, Georgia, which bore the portrait of the bank president, John E. Ward, a strong Union man, who had left the South early in the war.

The notes also depicted several public buildings in the South, numerous allegorical scenes, one scene from the Mexican War (a charge of Bragg's artillery) and a Revolutionary scene, in which Francis Marion entertains a British officer at a Spartan camp meal.

The printers and engravers who turned out the flood of money significantly insisted upon being paid for their work in gold. Most of the firms were those which produced stamps: Ludwig & Hoyer and Archer & Daly of Richmond, Keatinge & Ball and Evans & Cogswell of Columbia, South Carolina, J.T. Paterson of Augusta, Georgia.

Among minor producers were Colonel Blanton Duncan, who got engravers through the blockade from Europe and operated in Richmond and Columbia, and J. Manouvrier of New Orleans. The latter turned out some 15,000 notes of five-dollar denomination before dissatisfied Confederate agents canceled his contract, and the result is a rare item for collectors.

After August, 1862, Keatinge & Ball were the only official producers of Confederate notes (except for a fifty-cent note appearing later), but counterfeiters within and without the Confederacy were active until the end.

Modern prices of Confederate money are rising rapidly, as

of 1960, with many notes in fine condition being worth more than their face value.

The South seized three U.S. mints within her borders, but for lack of bullion did not get coins into circulation. The two coins which were struck have caused much confusion. As late as the 1950's these were still coming out of hiding, and the numbers of the pieces cannot be stated with accuracy.

The Confederate half dollar is the more famous coin. It was produced in the New Orleans mint in the spring of 1861 by the chief coiner, Dr. B.F. Taylor, with a design by A.H.M. Patterson. Its brief history:

A few United States half dollars of 1861 were found in the mint, and the reverse sides planed off and restamped (in a screw press) with Patterson's design. This featured a shield often used in United States designs, with seven stars over a field of stripes, the whole surrounded by the words "Confederate States of America," with a sprig of cotton and one of wheat as decoration. The legend at the bottom: "Half Dol."

The coin was unknown to collectors for many years, and until recently it was thought that but four of the "originals" had been struck—one given by Confederate Secretary of the Treasury C.G. Memminger to Jefferson Davis, one to Dr. Taylor, one to a Professor Biddle of the University of Louisiana, and another to a Dr. E. Ames of New Orleans.

Numismatists now believe that about a dozen were struck, since three have been sold in the market in the last few years; the last recorded sale of a Confederate half dollar as of early 1960 was in a Charlotte, North Carolina, auction. The price: $6,250.

In 1879 the firm of J.W. Scott of New York found the die and made "restrikes" by planing United States halves of 1861—500 in number. These now sell for upwards of $400 each.

The history of the "Confederate cent" is more spectacular. Robert Lovett of Philadelphia, a die cutter for a jewelry firm, contracted to make coins for the Confederacy before the outbreak of war.

He copied a design from his business card of 1860, the head of an Indian girl, and signed his name on the reverse as "L."

Lovett struck twelve of the coins in 1861, and became fearful that he would be discovered and imprisoned or executed for aiding the enemy. He buried the samples and the die in his cellar—except for one coin. In 1873, he inadvertently gave the coin to a saloonkeeper in change, and the proprietor notified an expert, Captain J.W. Haseltine, who recognized the piece as the work of Lovett. Haseltine investigated, bought the coins and die, and in 1874 had some restrikes made—seven in gold, twelve in silver, fifty-five in copper—at which point the die broke.

Recent catalogues value the gold restrike at $850, the silver at $350, and the copper at $300. The original pattern cent, in copper-nickel, was, curiously, valued at only $300.

Confederate Flags

The Bonnie Blue Flag seems to have been the first banner of Secession, and flew in Montgomery, Alabama, while the first Confederate Congress was in session. This flag, or something quite like it, had been used in the fight for the independence of Texas.

In 1861, at any rate, a song by this title made its debut in a New Orleans theater, written and sung by the entertainer, Harry MacCarthy. The first audience was composed largely of Texas volunteers on their way to battle.

This flag has a white star centered in a rectangular field of dark blue.

The Confederate Congress asked the public for flag designs, and got a bewildering variety, enough "to fill a big packing box." William Porcher Miles of South Carolina was chairman of the committee on flags.

A South Carolina woman wrote asking that the new nation date its life from Washington's Birthday, and call itself The Washington Republic. Another proposed the name Alleghania.

Many letters implored that the Stars and Stripes be used by the South; many more proposed the use of the Southern Cross.

The committee reported at length, and on March 4, 1861, the first "national," or official, Confederate flag was flown in Montgomery.

There is doubt as to the identity of the designer. One story credits Nicola Marschall, a Prussian musician and painter at the Marion Female Seminary, in Alabama, who is said to have dashed off three sketches in twenty minutes, when it appeared that the public offerings were not suitable. Marschall is also said to have designed the Confederate gray uniform.

Another story holds that the flag was designed by Major Orren Randolph Smith, of Louisburg, North Carolina, whose contribution was described in detail by witnesses.

The flag itself, also known as The Stars and Bars, has two horizontal stripes of red separated by a white stripe of equal width, and in the upper left corner a dark blue field with a circle of white stars. The first version had seven stars for the then-seceded states; a later version has thirteen.

The Stars and Bars went to war at First Manassas/Bull Run, and in the smoke and dust, as Confederate reinforcements came up, was mistaken for the United States flag. General P.G.T. Beauregard proposed a substitute, the now-familiar Battle Flag. The new banner was formally accepted in October, 1861, by Generals Beauregard, Joseph Johnston, and Earl Van Dorn before massed troops in a ceremony at Centerville, Virginia. The flags were the gifts of the leading Confederate belles, the Misses Cary—Constance, Hetty, and Jennie, patriotic seamstresses.

Though it never became an official flag, this "Red Cross Banner" was the true symbol of the Confederacy through most of the war. It was square, in various sizes for different services: infantry, 52 by 52 inches; artillery, 38 by 38; cavalry, 32 by 32. A rectangular flag of this design served the Confederate Navy as a jack.

In the Battle Flag the red square is crossed diagonally with two blue bars, and there are thirteen white stars on the blue.

In response to Beauregard's criticism, Congress created a second National Flag in May, 1863, the so-called Stainless Banner. This was a rectangle of white, with a small battle flag in the upper left corner.

This, too, had an unfortunate history, for it was more than once mistaken by the enemy for a flag of truce, when it hung limply.

On March 4, 1865, the final Confederate National Flag was adopted—The Stainless Banner with a vertical bar of red on the outer edge. The flag was not actually made at the time, since Congress was soon driven from Richmond; later examples were made on the basis of Confederate records.

The Great Seal

The Confederacy overlooked its need for a Great Seal with which to process documents until April, 1863, when Congress adopted one, specifying that the central figure should be a mounted George Washington. A surrounding wreath is fashioned of major Southern crops: cotton, corn, tobacco, sugar cane, wheat, and rice. The motto in the margin: "The Confederate States of America, Twenty-second February, Eighteen Hundred and Sixty-Two," followed by the motto, "Deo Vindice" (God will judge).

The design was followed with a single change, suggested by Secretary of State Benjamin, who made room for the lengthy message by using numerals for the date. (The date perpetuated the founding of the permanent Confederacy and inauguration of Jefferson Davis.)

James M. Mason, the Confederate commissioner in England, was ordered to have a seal made, with no expense spared to produce an artistic masterpiece.

The seal's creators were J.H. Foley, a British Sculptor, and Joseph S. Wyon, Chief Engraver to Her Majesty's Seals, whose shop was in London.

The seal and its equipment cost about $700.

It came to Richmond in a blockade-runner, brought by Lieutenant Robert T. Chapman of the Confederate Navy. Chapman gave it to Benjamin in August, 1864, but left the press behind in Bermuda, a way point in shipping the heavy device.

The press remained in the Darrell family of that island, and in 1960 its ownership had passed to a niece of the last Darrell, Ernest, deceased. Efforts were being made to have it placed in a museum. The seal, despite legends to the contrary, is in Richmond's Confederate Museum, where it has been on display for more than a generation.

Benjamin gave the seal to a clerk, William J. Bromwell, at the fall of Richmond, and Bromwell's wife smuggled it out in her clothing. It was moved to Charlotte, North Carolina, with State Department records, and in 1872 it changed hands.

Bromwell sold the records to the Federal Government for $75,000, and as reward, gave the seal and a commission to the helpful attorney who negotiated the sale, Colonel John T. Pickett. He had some electroplates of the seal made and sold them for the benefit of Confederate widows and orphans—and then passed the Seal to Lieutenant Thomas O. Selfridge, USN, who had aided the government in the purchase. Selfridge was sworn to secrecy as to the whereabouts of the seal.

For forty-seven years the Great Seal was lost to public view, and it was 1912 before Gaillard Hunt of the Library of Congress discovered it. Selfridge, by then an admiral, sold the seal to three prominent men of Richmond, Virginia (Eppa Hunton, Jr., William H. White, and Thomas P. Bryan) for $3,000 and they placed it in the Confederate Museum.

The seal is a massive silver circle about three and a half inches in diameter, with a thick ivory handle. It is displayed in its original velvet-lined leather box.

The seal was seldom, if ever, used officially during the war, since its weight made it difficult to use without a press. Reproductions are now familiar in the United States, these dating from 1873, when the first electroplates were made.

The authenticity of the seal now in Richmond was attested by Allen J. Wyon, who inherited the London engraving firm from his uncle. Wyon wrote:

> I have carefully examined the seal. . . . I have also compared it with the wax impression which has never left my studio, and I have no hesitation in stating that in my opinion there is no doubt that the seal which I have examined is the Great Seal of the Confederate States of America, which was engraved in silver by my uncle, Mr. J.S. Wyon, in the year 1864.

32

The Perfect Battle

ON Sunday, June 19, 1864, in the English Channel off Cherbourg, one turbulent hour brought to a climax the world-wide struggle for sea power between North and South.

The French cliffs, within sight, were lined with hundreds come to see the announced spectacle of the duel between the Yankee *Kearsarge* and the Rebel *Alabama*. The Frenchmen munched from food baskets as the drama unfolded.

These ships so far from home might have been twins, so far as the landsmen could see:

Kearsarge		*Alabama*
232'	length	220'
33'10"	beam	31'8"
16'	depth	17'
1,031	tonnage	1,050
400 h.p.	engines	300 h.p.

Certain differences in the guns, crews, armor, and ammunition could not be seen from shore. The Yankee's 11-inch guns outmatched those of her foe; her crew was all American, and larger, 163 to 149; her sides, amidships, were sheathed in metal chains, covered with boards. She had been in dock for repairs three months earlier, and her engines were in tune; her powder and shot were in good condition.

The skippers were not strangers come to grips. As seemed almost inevitable in this strange war, Raphael Semmes of the *Alabama* and John A. Winslow of the *Kearsarge* were friends

of many years, messmates, roommates, shipmates in old Navy—
and both Southerners.

As the ships moved into position, a French ironclad hovered
on the line of her territorial waters, within which American
fighting would be illegal. A French warship's band had played
Confederate music as the *Alabama* steamed out of harbor. There
was another neighbor, the English yacht *Deerhound*, which had
come to see the sport.

The yacht carried her wealthy owner, John Lancaster, his
wife, three sons, a daughter, and a niece. When they learned of
the impending fight the family took a vote, and the sea battle
had won over a trip ashore to church, only because the five-
year-old Lancaster son persuaded his sister, nine, to cast the
deciding vote. The youngster's thirst for spectacles of violence
saved the lives of some remarkable men.

The *Alabama* had been long on her way to this moment.
Built in Liverpool under subterfuge, christened by an anonymous
British beauty as *Enrica*, and variously known as "The 290" and
"The Emperor of China's yacht," she had almost literally swept
United States merchant shipping from the seas. In her twenty-
two months she had cruised 75,000 miles, equal to thrice around
the globe, had overhauled 295 vessels of all flags, taken 69 Yankees as prizes, and burned 54 which were valued at more than
five million dollars.

She had been fitted with guns in the Azores, and with her
large sails, her modern engines and a propeller which could be
raised for greater speed under sail, she caught almost every
quarry she sighted. Her graceful black hull bore no name, and
she was marked only by a motto on the stern in gilt letters:
Aide toi et dieu t'aidera. (Help yourself and God will help
you.)

She had fought and won, but was built for racing and prey-
ing on merchantmen. In all her months she had not changed her
black powder, which had become foul; in a firing test off South
America, not long before, most of her shells had failed to explode. Her bottom was foul, and her crew in poor discipline
after a long, discouraging run with few prizes. She had put in

at Cherbourg to repair and take on coal, and was delayed by red tape—Napoleon III could not be reached to grant asylum to the belligerent.

The *Kearsarge*, alerted at Flushing, had reached Cherbourg within two days, and made a bold circuit of the harbor, her officers inspecting the *Alabama* through glasses. The Yankee took her post just outside the harbor, and Semmes, with no other course open, announced that he would fight; escape by night would have further demoralized his international crew (mostly British, but including a Russian, Italians, Spaniards, Frenchmen, Irishmen, Dutchmen).

Raphael Semmes was fifty-three, a native of Maryland, a sailor since his midshipman days thirty-two years before. He had married a woman from Cincinnati, settled in Alabama, and was the father of two sons, both in the Confederate Navy.

He was by no means an idolized captain. "Old Beeswax," his prize crews called him; he had a steadfast habit of speaking to none but his senior officers, but his stern ways did not conceal his ability to handle men and ships, and the *Alabama* was efficiency itself through most of her career. He had volunteered for the important business of burning enemy commerce; there was now gray in his hair and long mustaches. Despite his glittering eyes which intimates found "fanatical," he looked more the part of an aging, slightly overweight master of a merchantman than the ogre of the seas so familiar in the Northern press.

He had a fetish about cleanliness and followed the best health practices, fearful of scurvy and other diseases; he carried two surgeons, and was careful of food and water for the crew. In after years, when offered coffee with canned milk, he was apt to explode and curse the substitute he had used at sea; then, if no fresh milk were available, he would dose his coffee with butter.

Cherbourg was crowded with sight-seers on Saturday night before the battle—all come to see the Americans in action. Hotels and homes were full. Water-front cafés were gay with farewell songs to the Confederate crew, which was rounded up early and taken aboard the *Alabama*. Semmes sent ashore the ship's valuables and had his men make their wills.

In the early morning Semmes seemed nervous. He astonished Lieutenant George Sinclair by speaking to him cordially, as an equal, asking him whether he thought they should go through with the battle. Sinclair reminded the captain of the foul bottom and the spoiled powder, but Semmes took little note of it; he had also passed over advice from the Port Admiral that he should not fight the *Kearsarge*, since she was sheathed in chain armor. The *Alabama* had chains in her hold, unused.

Semmes had the crew served a big breakfast and assembled them for one of his orations. He reviewed their career as destroyers of the American merchant marine and defenders of the Confederate flag, and pointed out that they would fight in the waters where their forebears (with some exceptions) had stopped the Spanish Armada. The gunners went to their posts, naked to the waist, Semmes and his officers appeared in their full-dress uniforms. Once under way, at 9:45 A.M., the cruiser passed a sizable fleet of French ships.

The *Alabama* ran into the channel with the French ironclad at her side. The *Kearsarge* was far ahead, some six or seven miles out, but she turned and bore down on the *Alabama* as if to ram her. Semmes turned aside; the *Alabama*, as usual, moved with agility, and a collision was avoided. Semmes went into a circle, and the ships moved thus, clockwise, with the original diameter of the circle about half a mile.

The current was westward, at three knots, and as the ships reduced the circle to 400 yards, coming to point-blank range, their field of battle drifted outward.

Semmes fired first, and missed, with a 100-pound shell from his chief weapon, a Blakely gun. *Kearsarge* returned a broadside and while the ships made seven turns of the circle, the guns hammered without ceasing and smoke often hid the vessels. Men ashore could note the difference in firing; the *Kearsarge* flashes were clear, and the *Alabama*'s cloudy and black. The Yankee gunners were superior almost from the start, and a hail of iron tore the Confederate decks, hull and rigging.

Even so, one of his first shots almost won the battle for Semmes—an 8-inch shell that by exquisite luck struck the wooden sternpost of *Kearsarge*, but did not explode. If it had gone off, ripping the stern from the ship, the Yankee could not have been steered, and would have lain at *Alabama*'s mercy as she maneuvered about. There was little else to cheer from the Rebel's decks, for of 370 shots fired, only fourteen hit the hull of the *Kearsarge*. On the other hand, Winslow's gunners shot for the waterline of the *Alabama*, and opened great holes.

Semmes soon told officers that their shot were bouncing off the sides of the *Kearsarge*, and that they should change their ammunition. The covered chain mail was highly effective under all types of fire.

The *Kearsarge* did such deadly work with her after pivot gun that Semmes offered a reward for its silencing and turned all his guns on it; the only result was the wounding of three men on the Yankee, her casualties for the day.

Semmes's deck was now littered with bodies, many badly mutilated; he had lost all but one of the eighteen-man crew at his own pivot gun. When he neared the end of the seventh circle, Semmes was told by his engineer that the boiler fires were out; the ship had about ten minutes to float, for rising water already threatened men below. Semmes tried several tricks at once: He pushed his guns to port to balance ship, but could get only one in position; he ran up the white flag, and spread a few yards of canvas in an effort to creep across the French territorial line where he would be immune from attack. The sailor sent up to loose the sail, John Roberts, was shot down, his abdomen torn open, and he fell shrieking to the deck.

Semmes was surrounded by men who shouted that they should not surrender, and some officers later recalled that they fired a few shots in defiance of the skipper's decision. The *Kearsarge*, at any rate, fired at least five rounds from her big guns after the white flag rose on the *Alabama*. Semmes sent a boatload of wounded to the *Kearsarge*, asking for boats to take off other survivors, but it happened that the Yankee's boats had been ruined in the fight, except for two. These two were sent, but were delayed.

On an order to abandon ship, and to get as far from her side as possible, the remaining crewmen jumped into the Channel; they were surprised to find its waters ice-cold. The *Alabama*'s one sound boat took off the wounded and picked up those who could not swim—though two of these died, unable to reach the boat.

French boats picked up a few men and, from the *Kearsarge*, Captain Winslow asked the *Deerhound* for help. Two boats from the yacht went to help survivors.

Semmes had a slight wound in one arm. He had help from

two men to pull off his boots, but declined to take off his trousers. He accepted a life belt, and with his senior officer, Lieutenant John M. Kell, he poised at the rail, where they flung their swords into the water and jumped. The *Alabama* went down by the stern, not far away. The guns careening down the deck helped her sink; great sobs seemed to come from the ship as water rushed into the hull and torrents of air bubbled up. The last sight of her was the sharp tip of her black bow, pointed upward.

Semmes, pulled from the water by a *Deerhound* boat, hid under a tarpaulin to avoid the enemy. Some men thought that Captain Winslow saw Semmes escape, but made no effort to catch his old friend, since he knew he would face almost certain execution if captured.

The *Deerhound* carried Semmes to England, where he had a royal welcome from British society, was entertained and offered money as if he were a native hero.

The *Alabama*'s casualties: nine killed, twenty wounded, twelve drowned.

Semmes left England to tour Europe, slipped through the blockade via Mexico into the Confederacy, and in the last months of the war commanded the locked-in fleet of ironclads in the James River. When Richmond fell, he was notified as an afterthought, blew up his fleet and marched his sailors like infantry on the route of retreat. He shortly found a locomotive, however, fired its boiler with wood from a picket fence, and was soon steaming westward in a makeshift train, picking up gray-clad hitchhikers as he went.

At Danville, where he met Jefferson Davis and a few troops, Semmes took part in plans for defense, and when he found his rank a handicap in the presence of army officers there, was created a brigadier general by the President—the only admiral-general in the Confederacy, and perhaps in history.

When Semmes surrendered at Greensboro, North Carolina, he made a point of accepting a written parole, giving his rank as both admiral and general. Later, when he was seized for trial as a pirate in defiance of this agreement, Semmes, a trained lawyer, made the plea that as a general officer he was immune from such prosecution. After a short stay in prison he won his point.

He returned to Mobile, but was not permitted to practice law, or fill a judgeship to which he was elected, since he had not been restored to citizenship and would not take a loyalty oath to the Union. He taught for a time at Alexandria, Louisiana, in a seminary whose prewar head had been William T. Sherman. Semmes gave up teaching, and after a brief try at editing a Memphis newspaper, returned to Mobile, where citizens gave him a house. He practiced law, remained aloof from Reconstruction politics, wrote his memoirs, and died of ptomaine poisoning in 1877, just short of his sixty-eighth birthday.

A reminder of the battle between the *Alabama* and *Kearsarge* is in the museum at Annapolis—the large section of oaken timber from the sternpost of the *Kearsarge*, in which is embedded the unexploded shell fired by Semmes's gunners—a round iron shot almost seven inches in diameter, weight 55 pounds. This souvenir was sent to President Lincoln by Captain Winslow on request. The fighting ship served the Navy until 1894, when she broke up on a reef in the Caribbean.

33

The Human Side of Robert E. Lee

GENERAL LEE, a legend in his lifetime as a symbol of The Lost Cause, became a mythical hero in death. Beneath the quiet, grand air of the Southern gentleman-general, of course, he was a human being—warm, affectionate, hot-tempered, and fallible.

No one seems to have understood him completely. Dr. Douglas Southall Freeman, his chief biographer, said, "I can account for every hour of Lee's life from the day he went to West Point until his death . . . but I never presumed to know what General Lee was thinking."

Long before the war, when Lee's children were young, he liked to tumble them into bed with him and read stories aloud. They had, however, to take turns tickling the soles of his feet, which he enjoyed. When the little ones tired, or became lost in the tales, Lee would pause: "No tickling, no story."

Years later, when Lee was at war, he got word of the death of his daughter Annie. His secretary saw him take the news without a change of expression, as he did the scores of other messages that day, but when the aide returned unexpectedly a few minutes later, he saw the general with his head on his camp desk, sobbing.

For months, at the height of the war, Lee had a pet hen which laid an egg under his cot each day—and he never forgot to leave the tent flap open for her. Lee saw to it that the hen traveled with the army, even on so fateful a campaign as the

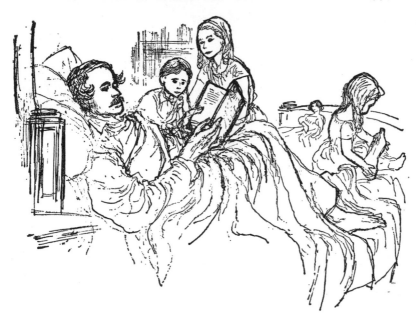

invasion which ended at Gettysburg. When he began the retreat from that field, and the hen was nowhere to be found, the commanding general joined the search for his pet, and was not content until she was discovered and safely perched in his headquarters wagon.

Lee's camp was usually crude and simple, and even when ground was unsuitable for his tents, he refused to disturb nearby residents by occupying their homes. Visitors were struck by his Spartan fare. He once entertained guests at a meal of cabbage upon which rested a single small piece of meat, a rarity in the field during the war. Each guest contented himself with cabbage, politely leaving the meat. The next day, when Lee asked his servant to use the meat for dinner, he got the reply: "We have no meat, General. That yesterday was borried middling."

The general's recreation was also simple. He often played chess, which was fashionable in both armies, and his favorite opponent was his aide, Colonel Charles Marshall. Their board was a pine slab, marked into squares with a knife by some headquarters artisan, the black squares inked in. The table was a tripod of pine branches cut from the woods.

Soldiers once watched him as he dismounted under fire at Petersburg to pick something from the ground and place it in a tree. When he had gone, the curious men found that he had replaced a fallen baby bird in its nest.

In the heavy firing of the opening battle of The Wilderness, a courier who dashed up to Lee with a dispatch was startled to get a scolding for having mistreated his horse by riding so swiftly. Lee then took a buttered biscuit from his saddlebag and fed the hungry animal before turning his attention to the battle.

On the morning of Appomattox Lee had at least a passing thought of suicide. He said within hearing of his staff: "How easily I could be rid of this, and be at rest. I have only to ride along the line and all will be over." But in the next breath he spoke of the people of the South, their bleak future, and the need to help their recovery.

One hot Sunday morning in 1864 Lee sat in a camp chair under a tree at Petersburg, joining some neighborhood ladies at church services. The preacher was his chief of artillery, the Reverend General W.N. Pendleton. One of the onlookers was an unknown private, the future poet, Sidney Lanier, who was stretched in the grass a few yards from the commander.

Lanier observed Lee fall asleep in the chair so soundly that a fly on his forehead did not wake him, nor did enemy shells bursting a few hundred yards away.

Lee was known for his self-control, but sometimes lost his temper. Once during the battles of the Seven Days, when General Jubal Early observed that the enemy were escaping, Lee exploded, "Yes, he will get away because I cannot have my orders carried out!"

At the battle of Chancellorsville he upbraided General Dorsey Pender: "That is the way you young men always do. You allow those people to get away. I tell you what to do, but you can't do it!'"

Yet despite almost constant disobedience to his orders by general officers, some of which was certainly insubordination, Lee left rare complaints on record, and there was never a suggestion of court-martial in such cases.

Lee's military secretary once noted that the general was irritated by having to sign numerous army papers; he gave telltale nervous jerks of his head. The secretary, also nettled, flung down the papers in wrath. Lee said calmly, "Colonel, when I lose my temper, don't let it make you angry."

Several officers reported, in varying fashion, Lee's loss of his temper, as at Gettysburg, when General J.E.B. Stuart reported belatedly with his cavalry. One general recalled, in later life, that the commander flushed and raised his hand as if he might strike the horseman. In every version of the story, however, Lee quickly regained his calm dignity and called on Stuart to do his best in the final phase of the battle.

After the war, when Lee was president of Washington College in Virginia, a friend saw him pause in a ride down a Lexington street to greet a woman friend on the sidewalk. Lee sat Traveller with his hat and reins in one hand, graciously making small talk.

The horse reared on hind legs several times, and came to earth in response to Lee's tugs. Unaccountably, Traveller continued to rear throughout the interview, a mystery to all except the observant friend across the street, who could see the General as he slyly dug the horse with his left spur, taking the occasion to indulge a small vanity over his horsemanship.

Lee's role as a firm, but gentle, patriarch endures in family traditions, including a favorite tale of his method of sounding curfew in his home.

In postwar Lexington, when young men from Washington College or cadets from Virginia Military Institute called on Lee's daughters, the General would emerge unfailingly into the

parlor from his study on the stroke of ten o'clock, and without
a word to the young people carefully draw the blinds and de-
part, signaling an uncompromising and faithfully observed farewell.

Lee may have come nearest to revelation of his inner con-
flicts in the terrible moments of the battle of Fredericksburg,
when Federal infantry was being cut to pieces by his guns from
impregnable hillside positions. Looking down, Lee said, "It is
well that war is so horrible, else we should grow too fond of it."

Lee endlessly goaded Richmond for adequate supplies and
clothing for his troops, but never permitted himself to scorn
the ragged scarecrows who marched with him. He came closest
when he told Francis Lawley, a British correspondent, "There
is only one attitude in which I never should be ashamed of your
seeing my men, and that is when they are fighting."

It was this Lee who commented to his son Custis, near the
end of the war, after a vain trip to Richmond to plead for help,
"I have been up to see the Congress, and they don't seem to be
able to do anything except eat peanuts and chew tobacco while
my army is starving."

Again, he said, "The only unfailing friend the Confederacy
ever had was cornfield peas."

Even in death Lee attracted homely incident. He died October 12, 1870, just two days after a flood had swept the hill
country. The Lexington undertaker, C.M. Koones, was embar-
rassed to report that he had no coffins, since the three he had
lately imported from Richmond had been swept away from his
river wharf.

Two young men—Charles H. Chittum and Henry Wallace—volunteered to search for a coffin for the Lee funeral.
They sought for hours before discovering one which had been
swept over a dam and had lodged on an island some two miles
downstream. Thus was provided the coffin in which the Confederacy's greatest figure was buried. The casket was too short
for Lee and he was buried without his shoes. (Lee was a small
man; his shoe size was four and a half.)

34

Aftermath-at-Arms

THE last shot of the Civil War was a blank.

It was fired eleven weeks and three days after Appomattox.

The scene was a most unlikely seascape—the ice-infested Bering Straits, at the entrance to the Arctic Ocean.

The sea was calm when a strange black-hulled steamer, heavily armed, came upon a fleet of Yankee whalers. It was June 28, 1865.

The big craft flew an American flag, but soon fired a warning blank, doffed her colors and ran up the true symbol of her trade, the Confederate flag.

The whaling ships had run afoul the fabled *Shenandoah* at the end of her eight-month career in which she had left a trail of burned U.S. shipping over some 60,000 miles. With the day's catch of eight burned ships and two captives, she ran her total to 38 ships and more than 1,000 men taken or destroyed in the Confederate cause. She did more than $1,000,000 in damage to the enemy.

Some of the whalers protested on the war's final day of action, and one captain, in his cups, threatened to fight the big raider alone with his little bomb gun, ordinarily used against whales. He was carried bodily from deck by his comrades, who had thoughtfully unloaded his gun in advance.

Five days earlier, burning a trading ship not far away, the *Shenandoah*'s skipper had been shown newspapers from San Francisco bearing accounts of Lee's surrender. The skipper was Captain James Iredell Waddell, a fighting man from North Carolina who limped from an old dueling wound. His eye had

caught other items in those newspapers, and they were enough
to send him against Federal shipping once more: Though Lee
had given up his army, Jefferson Davis issued defiant orders in
flight, and Colonel John Mosby vowed that he would never
surrender.

Waddell's career had been desperate in this ship from the
start; he pillaged with an international crew, in a craft stealthily
launched under false colors in England. One of his officers was
Sidney Smith Lee, Jr., nephew of Robert E.

Waddell burned the first whaler of his Arctic catch, the
Waverly, of New Bedford, Massachusetts, and turned to the
others. He spared one because of the tears of a widow, a Mrs.
Gray, of the *James Maury.* Captain Gray had died at sea, and

was packed in a whiskey barrel, preserved for burial at home. One more ship was tolled off to carry prisoners, and the others put to the torch.

Eight men were so taken by the *Shenandoah* that they signed on and sailed with the raider.

She bore down toward the California coast—now the object of a world-wide search pressed through the British Foreign Office at the insistence of James D. Bulloch, chief of Confederate secret service in Europe. Someone must find the *Shenandoah*, he said, and convince her that the war was over. Only the British Navy was so wide-ranging as to be likely to find her.

On August 2, Waddell hailed a British barque, the *Barracouta*, which was two weeks out of San Francisco, and asked how the war was going. When he learned that peace had broken out, Waddell sadly pulled his guns, put them below decks, and made for Liverpool. He reasoned that, since he was now defenseless, his chances of justice tempered with mercy might be better in a British court.

His navigator, Irvine Bulloch, took him the 17,000 roundabout miles to Liverpool in 122 days, without sight of land, and dropped anchor on November 4. On that day the last sovereign Confederate flag was furled for the last time.

With little stretch of the imagination, the boarding of the raider by admiring British officers may be considered the end of our Civil War.

The *Shenandoah*, a magnificent ship of 1,160 tons, with sails and a detachable screw propeller, had copper-sheathed teak planking, but she seemed to be no prize once she surrendered. One crew attempted to take her to America to be turned over to United States authorities, but her sails were torn in a storm and she was forced to turn back. She lay at dock in Liverpool for months until the Sultan of Zanzibar bought her for $108,000, about a quarter of the price the Confederates had paid for her.

She went into the tea trade, and during a storm in the Arabian Sea stove in her hull on a coral reef and sank with but a half-dozen survivors.

Waddell had one more battle left to him. Ashore, he took command of Maryland's Oyster Navy to enforce conservation laws in the Chesapeake, and with a crew of ten and two guns on his flagship, once met a fleet of oyster thieves in the bay. He sank one boat, drove three others ashore and captured three. It was his final fight before his death in 1886. The Maryland legislature adjourned in his memory.

35

The Price in Blood

AT least 618,000 Americans died in the Civil War, and some experts say the toll reached 700,000. At any rate, these casualties exceed the nation's loss in all its other wars, from the Revolution through Korea.

The Union armies had from 2,500,000 to 2,750,000 men. Their losses, by the best estimates:

Battle deaths: 110,070
Disease, etc.: 250,152
Total: 360,222

The Confederate strength, known less accurately because of missing records, was from 750,000 to 1,250,000. Its estimated losses:

Battle deaths: 94,000
Disease, etc.: 164,000
Total: 258,000

The leading authority on casualties of the war, Thomas L. Livermore, admitting the handicap of poor records in some cases, studied 48 of the war's battles and concluded:

Of every 1,000 Federals in battle, 112 were wounded.

Of every 1,000 Confederates, 150 were hit.

Mortality was greater among Confederate wounded, because of inferior medical service.

The great battles, in terms of their toll in dead, wounded, and missing:

GETTYSBURG

Union		*Confederate*
3,155	dead	3,903
14,529	wounded	18,735
5,365	missing	5,425
23,049	total	28,063

Grand total: 51,112. Duration, three days.

THE SEVEN DAYS

1,734	dead	3,478
8,062	wounded	16,261
6,075	missing	875
15,849	total	20,614

Grand total: 36,463. Duration, seven days.

CHICKAMAUGA

1,657	dead	2,312
9,756	wounded	14,674
4,757	missing	1,468
16,170	total	18,484

Grand total: 34,654. Duration, two days.

CHANCELLORSVILLE

1,575	dead	1,665
9,594	wounded	9,081
5,676	missing	2,018
16,792	total	12,764

Grand total: 29,556. Duration, four days.

SHARPSBURG/ANTIETAM

2,108	dead	2,700
9,549	wounded	9,024
753	missing	2,000
12,410	total	13,724

Grand total: 26,134. Duration, one day.

SECOND MANASSAS/BULL RUN

1,724	dead	1,481
8,372	wounded	7,627
5,958	missing	89
16,054	total	9,197

Grand total: 25,251. Duration, three days.

STONE'S RIVER/MURFREESBORO

Union		*Confederate*
1,677	dead	1,294
7,543	wounded	7,945
3,686	missing	2,476
12,906	total	11,795

Grand total: 24,701. Duration, two days.

SHILOH

1,754	dead	1,723
8,408	wounded	8,012
2,885	missing	959
13,047	total	10,694

Grand total: 23,741. Duration, two days.

FREDERICKSBURG

1,284	dead	595
9,600	wounded	4,061
1,769	missing	653
12,653	total	5,309

Grand total: 17,962. Duration, one day.

Some of the great blood baths of the war came as Grant drove on Richmond in the spring of 1864. Confederate casualties are missing for this campaign, but were enormous. The Federal toll:

> The Wilderness, May 5–7: 17,666.
> Spotsylvania, May 10 and 12: 10,920.
> Drewry's Bluff, May 12–16: 4,160.
> Cold Harbor, June 1–3: 12,000.
> Petersburg, June 15–30: 16,569.

These total 61,315, with rolls of the missing incomplete.

The Appomattox campaign, about ten days of running battles ending April 9, 1865, cost the Union about 11,000 casualties, and ended in the surrender of Lee's remnant of 26,765. Confederate dead and wounded in the meantime were about 6,500.

Lesser battles are famous for their casualties. At Franklin, Tennessee, November 30, 1864, General Hood's Confederates lost over 6,000 of 21,000 effectives—most of them in about two hours. Six Confederate generals died there.

Hood lost about 8,000 men in his assault before Atlanta, July 22, 1864; Sherman's Union forces lost about 3,800.

The small battle of Wilson's Creek, Missouri, August 10, 1861, was typical of the savagery of much of the war's fighting. The Union force of 5,400 men lost over 1,200; the Confederates, over 11,000 strong, lost about the same number.

The first battle of Manassas/Bull Run, though famous as the first large engagement, was relatively light in cost: 2,708 for the Union, 1,981 for the Confederates.

The casualty rolls struck home to families and regiments.

The Confederate General, John B. Gordon, cited the case of the Christian family, of Christiansburg, Virginia, which suffered eighteen dead in the war.

The 1st Maine Heavy Artillery, in a charge at Peterbsurg, Virginia, 18 June, 1864, sustained a "record" loss of the war— 635 of its 900 men within seven minutes.

Another challenger is the 26th North Carolina, which lost 714 of its 800 men at Gettysburg—in numbers and percentage the war's greatest losses. On the first day this regiment lost 584 dead and wounded, and when roll was called the next morning for G Company, one man answered, and he had been knocked unconscious by a shell burst the day before. This roll was called by a sergeant who lay on a stretcher with a severe leg wound.

The 24th Michigan, a gallant Federal regiment which was in front of the North Carolinians on the first day, lost 362 of its 496 men.

More than 3,000 horses were killed at Gettysburg, and one artillery battalion, the 9th Massachusetts, lost 80 of its 88 animals in the Trostle farmyard.

A brigade from Vermont lost 1,645 of its 2,100 men during a week of fighting in the Wilderness.

The Irish Brigade, Union, had a total muster of 7,000 during the war, and returned to New York in '65 with 1,000. One company was down to seven men. The 69th New York of this brigade lost 16 of 19 officers, and had 75 per cent casualties among enlisted men.

In the Irish Brigade, Confederate, from Louisiana, Company A dwindled from 90 men to 3 men and an officer in March, '65. Company B went from 100 men to 2.

Experts have pointed out that the famed Light Brigade at Balaklava lost only 36.7 per cent of its men, and that at least 63 Union regiments lost as much as 50 per cent in single battles. At Gettysburg 23 Federal regiments suffered losses of more than half their strength, including the well-known Iron Brigade (886 of 1,538 engaged).

Many terrible casualty tolls were incurred in single engagements, like that of the Polish Regiment of Louisiana at Frayser's Farm during the Seven Days, where the outfit was cut to pieces and had to be consolidated with the 20th Louisiana. In this action one company of the Poles lost 33 of 42 men.

One authority reports that of 3,530 Indians who fought for the Union, 1,018 were killed, a phenomenally high rate. Of 178,-975 Negro Union troops, this expert says, over 36,000 died.

Some regimental losses in battle:

Regiment	Battle	Strength	Per cent loss
1st Texas, CSA	Antietam	226	82.3
1st Minnesota, US	Gettysburg	262	82
21st Georgia, CSA	Manassas	242	76
141st Pennsylvania, US	Gettysburg	198	75.7
101st New York, US	Manassas	168	73.8
6th Mississippi, CSA	Shiloh	425	70.5
25th Massachusetts, US	Cold Harbor	310	70
36th Wisconsin, US	Bethesda Church	240	69
20th Massachusetts, US	Fredericksburg	238	68.4
8th Tennessee, CSA	Stone's River	444	68.2
10th Tennessee, CSA	Chickamauga	328	68
8th Vermont, US	Cedar Creek	156	67.9
Palmetto Sharpshooters, CSA	Frayser's Farm	215	67.7
81st Pennsylvania, US	Fredericksburg	261	67.4

Scores of other regiments on both sides registered losses in single engagements of above 50 per cent.

Confederate losses by states, in dead and wounded only, and with many records missing (especially those of Alabama):

North Carolina	20,602
Virginia	6,947
Mississippi	6,807
South Carolina	4,760
Arkansas	3,782
Georgia	3,702
Tennessee	3,425
Louisiana	3,059
Texas	1,260
Florida	1,047
Alabama	724

(Statisticians recognize these as fragmentary, from a report of 1866; they serve as a rough guide to relative losses by states).

In addition to its dead and wounded from battle and disease, the Union listed:

Deaths in prison	24,866
Drowning	4,944
Accidental deaths	4,144
Murdered	520
Suicides	391
Sunstroke	313
Military executions	267
Killed after capture	104
Executed by enemy	64
Unclassified	14,155

36

The War Is Not Over

ALMOST ninety-nine years lay between the deaths of the Civil War's first casualty and its last survivor.

The first man fell in May, 1861. By some accounts he was Colonel Elmer E. Ellsworth of the New York Fire Zouaves, slain May 24 by an irate Alexandria, Virginia, innkeeper after he had lowered a Rebel flag. By others, he was Private T.B. Brown, USA, who died from a Confederate bullet on May 22.

The identity of the "last man" is also uncertain, but the recognized final survivor was Walter Williams, once a forager for John Hood's Texans, who died in Houston on December 19, 1959, at the age of 117. He was counted the last of the war's four millions, outliving the last Union veteran, Albert Woolson of Duluth, Minnesota, by about three years.

The long reach of the war's history has kept it alive in the nation's modern era and prompted a unique revival.

In the week of Williams's death the nuclear submarine *Robert E. Lee* was launched on a missile-firing career while troops in Confederate uniform stood to the strains of "Dixie."

The Late Unpleasantness caused a tense moment during the 1959 visit of Nikita Khrushchev to Washington.

The Russian guest was momentarily expected at Blair House when a car arrived at headquarters of the Civil War Centennial Commission next door. A cargo of muskets, swords, and grenades was being unloaded when soldiers and secret service men sprang for the perspiring official.

"What's going on?"

"Nothing. General Grant's going on television, and these are his props."

"Guns!"

"Sure—all Civil War issue."

The security police retreated into their own century amid the smiles of amused spectators.

The Grant involved was Ulysses S. III, a retired army general. He was by no means the only bearer of a distinguished Civil War name in the 1960's.

Robert E. Lee IV is a San Francisco advertising man. J.E.B. Stuart III is an engineer with Consolidated Edison in New York. John C. Pemberton III practices law in New York. Bedford Forrest III lost his life in World II in a bombing mission over Germany. George E. Pickett III died in June, 1959. A retired Veterans' Administration official and leader of the Civil War Round Table movement, he was not only the grandson of the Confederate who gave his name to the war's most famous charge; another grandfather was on General Meade's staff at Gettysburg, in blue.

Others are legion, among them:

Philip St. George Cooke, Richmond, Virginia; Colonel Sidney Smith Lee, US Marine Corps, Retired; William Henry French, and Dr. Hayden Kirby Smith, of Washington, D.C.; William B. Taliaferro, of Norfolk, Virginia; Colonel Henry Jackson Hunt, USA, retired, of Bradenton, Florida; Benjamin Franklin Cheatham III, of Walkerton, Virginia; Major John Alexander Logan, of Tuscon, Arizona; George Gordon Meade III, of Ambler, Pennsylvania.

There is also Dr. Richard D. Mudd, US Air Force, Retired, practicing physician in Saginaw, Michigan, the grandson of Dr. Samuel Mudd, who was imprisoned for giving aid to John Wilkes Booth after Lincoln's assassination. The doctor was still trying, in 1960, to clear his grandfather's name.

George S. Patton, Jr., the famed commander of the 7th and 3rd US Armies in World War II, was the son and grandson of Virginia Military Institute professors who bore the same name; his grandfather was killed in battle at Winchester, Virginia, in

June, 1864, as Colonel of the 22nd Virginia and commander of a brigade.

In short, the war goes on, in more than memory.

General Grant found himself in one of 1959's liveliest squabbles after approving publication of a charge that the Civil War was fomented by international Jewish interests, especially the House of Rothschild.

A fury of newspaper headlines followed, with the Anti-Defamation League of B'nai Brith protesting loudly. General Grant replied that anti-Semitism had not occurred to him in the matter, and he had rather casually approved circulation of the tale to the Military Order of the Loyal Legion of the US, composed of the sons of Union veterans. Grant later branded the charge against the Jews as false in its entirety.

As the war's centennial approached, sales of Confederate flags rivaled those of Old Glory. Many of America's World War II enemies could recall the strange Stars and Bars which had flown in battle. As long ago as 1942 a Marine fighter squadron on Guadalcanal had billed itself as CONFORSOLS (Confederate Forces of the Solomons).

In the Korean War young Southerners of the Seventh Marines, in H Company of the Third Battalion, flew a Confederate flag on the front lines for months, and saw it shot down four or

five times. When its owner was wounded, the banner accompanied him to a hospital, and failed to survive an accidental fire.

A private of the company, C.R. Sanders, wrote to the United Daughters of Confederacy in Murfreesboro, Tennessee, explaining the emergency. He was soon flying a replacement.

A hero of the Marines in Korea was General Lewis B. (Chesty) Puller, who played a major role in the retreat from Chosin Reservoir. Puller is a grandson of one of Jeb Stuart's cavalry officers who was killed at Kelly's Ford. His grandmother died after a ten-mile walk in a snowstorm when Federal troops burned her house, having found her husband's spurs on a wall and classed them as war equipment.

Ancient Fort Macon on the North Carolina coast was occupied by US troops in World War II, for the first time since its capture from Confederates in 1862. Fireplaces provided the only heat, and some unsuspecting soldiers rolled cannon balls into position as andirons, mistaking them for solid iron shot. The powder-filled balls exploded, killing two men and injuring others. A syndicated newspaper cartoon headlined the tragedy:

CONFEDERATE SHELL KILLS TWO YANKEE SOLDIERS
80 YEARS AFTER IT WAS FIRED

A chapter of the United Daughters of The Confederacy flourishes in Paris. Liverpool is the home of the Confederate Research Council.

The wife of the Lord Mayor of London (1960), the Honorable Lady Stockdale, is a great-granddaughter of General John C. Breckinridge, the eminent Confederate.

Lady Nancy Astor, a Native Virginian, made headlines in her eighties with her barbed quip on American sectionalism: "I'd rather be a rattlesnake than a Yankee."

Today's casual newspaper readers see frequent reminders of the War of the Sixties: Senator Stuart Symington of Missouri is the namesake of his grandfather, an officer on Pickett's staff at Gettysburg. Young Harmon Killebrew, an American League homerun king, is descended from the Union army's "finest physical specimen" from Illinois. Bernard Baruch, the Wall Street magician and park-bench statesman, is the son of a physician who served four years as a doctor in gray.

In 1927, when Harry Flood Byrd was Governor of Virginia, a well-preserved Virginia flag was returned to its home. Its donor was Frederick A. Stevens of Melrose, Massachusetts, today a retired Marine Corps general. Stevens is the grandson of the man who tore the Virginia flag from its staff atop the Capitol on April 3, 1865—Major Atherton H. Stevens, provost marshal of a Federal corps and one of the first men in blue to enter the fallen city. Stevens climbed to the top of the building, removed the flag, and replaced it with guidons of his cavalry outfit, the 4th Massachusetts. In the generations thereafter the captive flag, which had been made by patriotic Richmond women, was given the best of care by the major, his son, and his grandson.

The very surname of the striking modern American hero, Charles A. Lindbergh, has a Civil War background. One Mäns Olsson, a great uncle, invented the name now used by the great aviator. Olsson took the name Lindbergh while attending a Swedish school, to avoid confusion over the family's identity. Mäns migrated to America in 1862 with his brother Charles, grandfather of the future conqueror of the Atlantic. Mäns fought with the 82nd Illinois, but Charles did not see service.

In August, 1956, a Swedish bank teller cheerfully changed a $500 Confederate banknote for an enterprising customer, at the same favorable rate of exchange commanded by Federal currency in that season. His mistake was discovered only when it was much too late.

The growth of a small industry in the sale of relics and mementos of the Civil War has been a phase of the Boom. Almost all of the worth-while books on the conflict have been reprinted within the past five years, many of war date and including highly specialized works like atlases, sketches of uniforms and arms. New volumes pour forth. Autographs, letters, and documents, especially those of leading figures like Lincoln and Lee, command prices out of proportion to other American historical material.

A growing army of treasure hunters, using mine detectors, covers the battle areas outside the national parks—and sometimes raid within the boundaries. A Park Ranger at Chancellorsville nabbed three suspects with a mine detector who strayed onto Federal land in 1958, and only after long consultation was persuaded to withhold the majestic force of The Law; his victims were Archie K. Davis of Winston-Salem, N.C., the chairman of the board of the South's largest bank, an inveterate Civil War Buff, and his two sons, aged eight and ten.

General Lee's wartime cook was Captain Joel Compton of Gretna, Virginia, a burly young man billed as the champion wrestler of the Army of Northern Virginia. A lively tradition among his descendants is that Joel inflicted the final casualty upon Grant's forces when he killed a bluecoat in a wrestling match following the surrender at Appomattox.

Captain Compton lived until 1932, at ninety still defiantly Confederate.

One of his great-grandsons was still "in uniform" as the war's centennial drew nigh: James I. (Bud) Robertson, Jr., Ph.D, editor of a scholarly journal published by the University of Iowa, *Civil War History*.

The United States hanged one "war criminal"—the Swiss-born physician, Henry Wirz, a Richmond prison clerk who became head of the infamous Andersonville prison in Georgia. The condemned victim, when the sentence was read, said, "I'm damned if the Yankee eagle hasn't turned out to be what I expected, a damned turkey buzzard."

A lifelong infidel, he was attended by Catholic priests at the end, Fathers Boyle and Wigget, and affirmed his belief in immortality of the spirit. He was hanged November 10, 1865, before an audience of two hundred in the Old Capitol prison yard and an auxiliary of thousands perched on rooftops overlooking the walls.

There was a long wait while the priests murmured with Wirz, and the officer in charge, Major George B. Russell, read the charges. In the lulls there was shouting from the impatient crowds on the rooftops, and the priests calmed the uneasy Wirz as he looked about him: "Faith, hope, charity, and repentance will save you."

Major Russell made ready to slip a black cap over the head of the criminal. "Have you a last word?"

"I have nothing to say to the public," Wirz said. "But to you I say I am innocent. I can die but once. I have hope for the future."

Wirz solemnly shook hands with the major. "Thank you for your courteous treatment, sir," he said.

Russell fixed the cap on the head of the doomed man, and the roar of the outer crowd rolled over the yard. Russell lifted his cap in signal, a drop opened in the gallows floor, and Wirz fell on the end of his rope. His body jerked in spasms for seven minutes, Russell saw by his watch, and after a quarter of an hour the body was taken down.

Doctors "dissected" the corpse in the night, and determined that the neck was not broken. Wirz was buried in the arsenal yard near the graves of the Lincoln conpirators.

In 1869 Wirz was reinterred in Mount Olivet Catholic Cemetery in Washington, his grave marked by a small simple stone reading: "Wirz."

In 1960 an addition had been made, obviously of recent vintage. A companion stone reads: "Captain, C.S.A. Martyr." This is said to be the contribution to history of an anonymous sympathizer from South Carolina.

In contrast is a monument to Wirz at Andersonville, which bears the text of General Grant's letter refusing the exchange of prisoners. The other side offers a prediction by Jefferson Davis: "When time shall have softened passion and prejudice, when Reason shall have stripped the mask from representation, then Justice, holding evenly her scales, will require much of the past censure and praise to change places."

Hundreds of men clad in authentic Federal and Confederate uniforms practice industriously these days, as members of the North-South Skirmish Association. Their crack musket teams, firing Civil War arms, with black powder and old-fashioned lead balls, almost invariably outshoot American service teams equipped with the most modern rifles. Their semiannual shoots attract thousands to the colorful spectacles which are almost as noisy as the war they commemorate. Civil War cannon provide lively background music.

37

Atrocities

IN 1862, when a Federal column drove deep into the South, the Russian-born General John B. Turchin took the town of Athens, Alabama. His leading companies drove out defending Confederate troops, and for a few minutes civilians fired on the invaders.

When occupation was complete, Turchin assembled his cavalrymen in the town square and in his heavy accents advised them on Total Warfare: "Now, boys, you stops in this Rebel town this night and I shut mine eyes for von hours."

Soon afterward, seeing no signs of trouble, Turchin sent for his adjutant to ask if the place was being set afire. When the soldier reported that there had been no arson, Turchin said insistently, "Well, tell the boys I shut mine eyes for von hours and a half."

At last the troopers fell to the work, burned and looted the town. There were numerous reports of atrocities committed there, including rapine.

Turchin fell into disrepute when the story was circulated and he was court-martialed and dismissed from the service. His charming wife, however, was yet to be reckoned with. "Mama" had already come to fame by commanding the regiment in battle when her husband was wounded. She took her case to Washington, and by a personal plea to Lincoln had Turchin restored to command, and advanced in rank.

Like most atrocity stories of the war, this is to be taken at something less than face value, but the cited facts are accepted as accurate in general.

The University of Alabama was burned by Federal troops in April, 1865, despite the eloquent protests of the Professor of French, André Deloffre.

Commander of the raiding party, General J.T. Croxton, admitted that it was a pity to burn the institution, but was under orders to destroy it, and it went up in flames, including the library.

Professor Deloffre's residence was spared because he flew the French flag over it.

Confederate guards are said to have massacred several Germans who were being escorted into Mexico under a proclamation ordering nonsympathetic citizens banished from Texas. In a brief encounter the Germans lost nineteen dead and nine wounded—the latter soon murdered.

Survivors joined the United States 1st Texas Cavalry, a crack outfit which fought gallantly for three years.

A Federal lieutenant, Joseph E. Osborn, reported the case of a sutler of his acquaintance, who was caught by Confederates after he had been selling goods to Union troops. Osborn said, "Though he begged for mercy on his knees, he was chopped to pieces until there remained no piece larger than his head."

In a similar case a Federal officer, Colonel Robert L. McCook of the 9th Ohio, lost his life when Confederate guerrillas caught him as he rode, wounded, in an ambulance. The wagon was overturned by the attackers and McCook was shot in cold blood.

The more familiar tales of atrocities during the war include the alleged slaughter of Negroes at Fort Pillow by Confederates—and the more fully authenticated incident at the battle of the Crater.

The latter case, in July, 1864, before Petersburg, climaxed the attempt of the 48th Pennsylvania regiment—or a few of its miners—to break Lee's lines with a 500-foot tunnel, by blowing up fortifications with a huge charge of powder.

In a confused attack following the explosion, Federal regiments were crowded into a narrow opening, the lead files went down into the vast crater left by the explosion, and at last a Negro division was pushed forward.

A Confederate counterattack directed by General William Mahone stopped the Federals and Southern troops surrounded the rim of the crater, slaughtering the helpless Negroes beneath them. Men in the front ranks shot until ammunition was gone, were handed muskets from the rear, and then turned to spearing their victims by hurling the bayoneted arms downward.

By tradition, at least, General R.E. Lee sent an order that the slaughter must cease, or Mahone would be removed from command.

Eyewitness accounts, even on the Confederate side, attest to the truth of charges concerning these killings.

On the other hand, Federals were charged with bayoneting the captured Confederate sick at Belmont on the Mississippi, and the 2nd Tennessee, CSA, an Irish regiment, was with difficulty restrained from swimming the river at Columbia, Tennessee, to get at the enemy.

Warfare in Northern Virginia was never more bitter than between the horsemen of George Custer and John S. Mosby. Stung by the successful raids of Mosby's rangers, who were considered bushwhackers, the Federals tried extreme measures.

Mosby was so successful in raiding Federal supply lines that Secretary of War E.M. Stanton wired General Grant that to open the Manassas railroad line, vital to a final offensive, they must "clean out Mosby's gang who have long infested that district. . . . The Thirteenth and Sixteenth New York Regiments under General Augur have been so often cut up by Mosby's band that they are cowed and useless for that purpose."

At Berryville, Virginia, in August, 1864, a force of 3,000 Federals was escorting a wagon train to the front when 300 of Mosby's men fell upon them and with the aid of two small cannon scattered their cavalry, rode through the infantry, captured and burned the wagons, and stole all the horses.

Soon afterward Grant ordered his cavalry chief, Philip

Sheridan: "When any of Mosby's men are caught, hang them without trial."

On September 23, when about eighty Rangers attacked a larger Federal force at Front Royal, six of the Confederates were captured. Four of these men were publicly shot in the streets of the town. Two others were offered freedom if they would lead Federal troopers to Mosby's headquarters. When they refused, these two men were hanged, and placards were pinned on their bodies as they swung from a large walnut tree: "Such will be the fate of all of Mosby's men." Another Ranger was caught some three weeks later, and hanged in nearby Rappahannock County.

In retaliation, Mosby, when he captured twenty-seven of Custer's men, had them draw lots. He shot two and hanged four, then wrote Sheridan details of their deaths. This brought the executions to an end.

The fate of Columbia, South Carolina, has been in controversy from the day Sherman's troops marched through, and flames swept the city. An example of the partisan furor which has raged since is the title of a book by an eyewitness, Dr. D.H. Trezevant, of Columbia: *The Burning of Columbia, S.C.: A Review of Northern Assertions and Southern Fact.*

Of Sherman, Trezevant wrote: "The utter devastation of the whole country from Columbia to North Carolina, makes him one of the most ruthless invaders that ever cursed the earth by his presence. Attila or Alaric shrink into insignificance when compared with him."

The novelist, William Gilmore Simms, whose account of Federal behavior was more temperate, said, "We have heard of some few outrages, or attempts at outrages, of the worst sort, but the instances in the case of white females have been very few."

Negro women, especially in the surrounding countryside, Simms reported, were "horribly" used. "Regiments in successive relays subjected scores of these poor women to the torture of their embraces. . . . Horrid narratives of rape are given which we dare not attempt to individualize."

He did write of one Negro woman, raped in Columbia by invading soldiers, who drowned her in a mud puddle. Simms added that Federal troops opened new graves in search of jewels and other valuables, and when they found more horses and mules than they could use, cut their throats. One pile of forty mule corpses was reported on the Saluda River.

Soldiers of both armies were notoriously thorough foragers, and in most marches left the country picked clean behind them. In the Western theater, after Shiloh, Southern plantation owners who complained bitterly that they were being ruined by looters were told ominously: "Just wait until the 8th Missouri comes along."

On the Confederate side General Joseph Wheeler's cavalry had a peerless reputation for living off the country, at the expense of Confederate or Federal civilians. Many Southern victims claimed that Yankee invaders were mere amateurs by comparison.

In 1864, when Federal warships bombarded Charleston, South Carolina, the defenders sought to hamper the attack by warning that they would take fifty Union soldiers from prison and expose them to the fire. The Union commander, General John G. Foster, retaliated by ordering fifty Confederate prisoners of equal rank shipped down from Johnson's Island. These included five generals, fifteen colonels, fifteen lieutenant colonels and fifteen majors. The list was published in newspapers, and the scheduled event became a national entertainment.

After spending weeks in a prison ship near Charleston, sometimes suffering in heat as high as 130 degrees below decks, these prisoners were exchanged. The anticlimax to the affair came as boats bearing the two bands of prisoners met in Charleston Harbor, amid laughter and banter.

Most of the war's familiar tales of atrocities centered about prisons on both sides. Andersonville is well known as a death pen, but it appears that suffering at Camp Douglas and other Northern prisons was on the same scale. In the relatively obscure

Confederate prison at Salisbury, North Carolina, almost 12,000 Federals are buried in a space the size of a football field.

In many atrocity stories war hysteria is obvious, and the authenticity of many is in doubt. For example:

The Confederate writer, D.G. deFontaine, under the name "Personne," reported that a Mrs. L.S. Hall, wife of a legislator from Wetzel County, West Virginia, was forced to parade in the streets of New Martinsville with her clothing tied over her head. The account added: "Report says that an outrage to which death is preferable was perpetrated upon her person. The Yankee hellhounds afterwards burned down Mr. Hall's house."

38

The Folklore

A STRIKING byproduct of the war was a rich outpouring of folk tales, some cast in the mold of classic legend. Even a sampling reflects the American preoccupation with the conflict which has endured from Fort Sumter to the Centennial. This preoccupation is never more colorful than when it plays about the chief figures of the War of Brothers.

A lingering legend is that Abraham Lincoln was the son of a mountaineer (Kentuckian or North Carolinian, in various versions), at whose home Nancy Hanks lived briefly.

This tale has more than once reached the dignity of treatment in books, and many people in the hill country profess to believe it today. According to this story, Nancy Hanks, who spent some years in the North Carolina hills, remained for months in the home of Abraham Enloe, in western North Carolina, on a main wagon route to the west.

She became pregnant by the master of the house, and was banished by Mrs. Enloe. The master of the wagon train taking her West was Thomas Lincoln, to whom she was soon married. Lincoln is said to have agreed to accept the paternity of the child who was to become the most renowned American of his era.

A book by James A. Cathey claimed, on the basis of interviews with elderly mountain people held just before 1900, that the Enloe story was true. Photographs stress the resemblance of face and figure between Lincoln and his "half brother," Wesley

Enloe, those of the latter made at the age of eighty-one. The "evidence" ends there.

The dates given do not bear out this tale, for Kentucky documents make it certain that Abraham Lincoln was born three years after Nancy Hanks married Thomas Lincoln. Citation of these facts by biographers has not checked the popularity of the story in the Southern mountains.

Other versions of the Enloe story are laid in various parts of Kentucky. Among even more unlikely tales are those crediting the siring of Lincoln to John C. Calhoun, to a stepson of Chief Justice John Marshall, to Henry Clay, and even to Patrick Henry, who died a decade before Lincoln's birth. This is in the familiar vein of ancient folklore, in which the parentage of great men is attributed to distinguished men on the ground that the common people, as represented in this case by the Hanks-Lincoln strain, cannot produce an Abraham Lincoln.

There is the birth legend of Robert E. Lee, which, though given no attention by biographers or historians, remains popular and is accepted as fact by many. This is the tale that Lee was born "after the death of his mother," some versions declaring that Mrs. Lee was actually in her coffin when a servant heard her groan and saved her from being buried alive. Soon afterward, by this version, she gave birth to Robert E. Lee.

The accepted facts are that Anne Carter Lee bore the fourth child of Lighthorse Harry Lee at Stratford, the ancestral home. on January 19, 1807, and that the result of normal childbirth was Robert E. Lee. The only illness on record for Mrs. Lee in this period is a severe cold she caught while riding in an open carriage a few days before the birth.

Robert, in any event, was born in a room said to have been the birthplace of two signers of the Declaration of Independence, Richard Henry Lee and Francis Lightfoot Lee.

John Wilkes Booth was, almost beyond the possibility of a doubt, killed in a tobacco farm at the home of Richard Garrett, near Port Royal, Caroline County, Virginia, on April 26, 1865. He was shot in violation of orders by Sergeant Boston Corbett, a religious fanatic who collected $1,653.85 in reward for his deed and was later clapped into an insane asylum after he tried to wipe out the Kansas legislature with two pistols.

Lincoln's assassin was hardly dead before legends sprang up. At least twenty men in the two generations afterward claimed to be Booth. One, bearing the aliases John St. Helen and David E. George, was a suicide in Enid, Oklahoma, in 1903; he told friends he was the escaped Booth. His body was taken to Memphis, Tennessee, by a believer, and for many years was exhibited as a mummy in shows touring the country.

An eminent Southern minister, the Reverend J.G. Armstrong, was thought by members of his congregations in Richmond and Atlanta to be Booth; and Edwin Booth, brother of John, was said to have been so stunned by the resemblance between Armstrong and his brother as to seek a private audience with him. The preacher died in 1891, but he lives in legend, with many believers convinced of his role in Lincoln's tragic end.

About half a dozen skulls have been exhibited as those of Booth, and offered for sale to museums.

Most of these tales may be traced to the almost unbelievably bizarre behavior of those two chief characters in the capture and death of Booth—Secretary of War Edwin Stanton, and the soldier-detective, Lafayette Baker.

Booth was cornered in the barn with Davy Herold, a feeble-minded boy soon to be hanged as one of the Lincoln conspirators. Herold came from the barn and surrendered on command, and at first said he did not know his companion, though Federal authorities said he later changed his story, and identified Booth.

Booth's body was thrown into a wagon, and under an escort of soldiers taken to the nearby Rappahannock to await a steamer. The wagon broke down, tumbling the bloody corpse to the ground and frightening the Negro driver so that he left the procession. In Washington, where detectives and soldiers squabbled for the $75,000 reward, Booth's body went through a remarkable process:

It went by tug to the ironclad *Montauk*, which lay in the Potomac with Booth's fellow conspirators chained in the hold. The body lay in the sun all day. Colonel Baker declared it to be

Booth's, but these mysterious circumstances prompted gossip in the city that day that Booth had not been captured, and that the Government, to conceal its failure, dared not show the body.

In response Stanton sent a coroner's jury of sorts to examine the body—all from his own staff except two, a hotel clerk who knew Booth by sight, and Dr. John F. May, who had once removed a tumor from Booth's neck.

The announced identification by this jury did not sate public curiosity. Thousands lined the bank of the Potomac to stare at the ironclad; one party got aboard, and only by main strength did Colonel Baker force one woman to surrender a hank of hair cut from the corpse. By night, in fear that the body was becoming a symbol which would somehow resurrect the Confederacy, Stanton had Baker take it into a skiff and row it downriver to a swampy area where the bodies of army horses and mules had been thrown. The throng on the banks kept pace for miles, splashing and shouting, keeping the skiff within sight until near the end.

At midnight the skiff crept back, and through a newly opened hole in an old prison building, the body was smuggled from public view. As an army physician and four soldiers watched, the coffin was buried in a warehouse floor. Rumors grew more fantastic after the trial and execution of the Lincoln conspirators.

Within two months Dr. May felt a need to reassert his positive identification of Booth's body, but caused further confusion by his statement that at first glance he had been unable to recognize the man as Booth, and that only the scars on the neck had convinced him. There were already reports that Booth had been seen, very much alive, in various parts of the country, and in South America as well.

Almost four years later, in February, 1869, in a futile effort to lay the ghosts, the Government dug up the body and turned it over to the Booth family. Edwin Booth could not bear to look at the remains, but had friends inspect it for him, including a nameless dentist who was said to have recognized the teeth as those of John Wilkes Booth. No details were given, and the pub-

lic remained unsatisfied, even as to whether the body was placed
in an unmarked grave in Baltimore's Greenmount Cemetery, as
the family claimed.

A Baltimore newspaper gave rumors a last fillip by reporting that one of its men had witnessed the macabre scene, and
noticed that the right leg of the corpse had been broken, and not
the left, as Booth's was supposed to have been.

A lively tale which must be classed as folklore despite the
insistence of its protagonist that it was a real-life drama, is the
saga of Loleta Velasquez. This adventuress said she was descended from the explorer who pioneered in Mexico and established a family tradition.

Loleta, by her own testimony, had a New Orleans tailor design a wire net to disguise her formidably feminine figure, and
in Confederate uniform and impeccable male disguise, raised,
equipped and paid for a Confederate regiment. She studied army
regulations, managed the training of her troops, and took them
by train to Pensacola, where she presented them to her astonished
husband.

This worthy aided in the further training until he was accidentally killed; Loleta assumed command once more and led
the regiment through a series of battles as an independent force,
the basis for her rather breathless book of reminiscences.

Loleta also performed as a spy, slipping through Federal
lines at will, but later became a Confederate soldier, as Lieutenant
Harry T. Buford. She also served on a blockade-runner, and survived to enjoy three marriages and raise four children.

The deaths of generals in battle created a spate of folk tales,
some of them with the ring of truth, but now beyond the reach
of the historian's tests. Typical is the story of General John F.
Reynolds, USA, the gifted corps commander who fell at Gettysburg.

On the first day of the fighting, Reynolds directed the attack of the Iron Brigade which eventually drove General Archer's men from McPherson's Woods, captured Archer and many

of his troops, and drove the force across Willoughby Run. Just as the success of the thrust became apparent, Reynolds was felled by a sharpshooter.

The bullet struck him in the neck, and Reynolds shouted a last order to his men to hurry forward, then fell into the arms of an aide, a Captain Wilcox. "Good God, Wilcox, I am killed," were his last words.

Some years after the war, when Pennsylvania was building a large granite monument to her dead, a state official visited the quarry at Mount Airy, North Carolina, where the work was being done. The monument included a number of white columns, with statuary to be mounted outside.

The Pennsylvanian instantly recognized one figure.

"That's General Reynolds," he said.

"Yes," said his Tar Heel guide, "and there's the man who killed him." He pointed to a workman in a nearby shed.

The workman was Frank Wood, who told the visitor: "I went up to Gettysburg with our army, and the first day we got separated from our company—Private Cox and I. We got into a railroad cut, and then climbed out under a rail fence. There was fighting all around.

"In front of us, a few hundred yards away, we saw a Yankee officer on a big horse, with lots of gold braid about him. He was standing in his stirrups and yelling to his boys: 'Give 'em hell, boys. Give 'em grape.'

"Cox asked if I could hit him, and I said I thought I might. I raised the sights on my musket and fired, and knocked him off the horse. I didn't know who he was at first. They told us afterward."

Wood had returned to the North Carolina hills after the war, to make and sharpen tools used in working stone in the quarry.

It was in the quarry that he made the tools which fashioned the white granite Pennsylvania monument, upon which stood the figure of the general he had killed.

Stonewall Jackson's talented engineer, the untutored Claiborne R. Mason, created a small body of folklore on his own.

This Virginian confessed that he never learned to read or write, beyond the laborious tracing of his signature, but he made a fortune as a contractor. Mason graded and laid most of the railroad track of the old Virginia Central along the modern Chesapeake and Ohio route between Washington, Charleston and Cincinnati.

His method of computation involved a tiny pocket rule, with which he could sight a hillside or grade and accurately estimate the amount of earth to be moved. This son of a poor Shenandoah Valley farmer became boss of construction gangs, then a wealthy contractor.

Mason attached himself to General Jackson early in the war, with civilian status, and helped the little valley army toward fame. Though Jackson often had general officers under arrest for what he considered insubordination, Mason went his own way.

Jackson once called a meeting of his officers, and Mason was nowhere to be found. Since he required the engineer's advice, the general sent an orderly in search of him. Mason was discovered in camp, cooking turnip greens for his supper. To the peremptory command that he report to General Jackson, Mason replied, "Son, you tell the general I'll be there in fifteen minutes."

The orderly insisted, but got no more than the promise that Mason would report when the greens were done, and had been consumed. The orderly went with some trepidation to Jackson, fearing that a court-martial would be called.

Instead, Jackson heard the news without comment, and waited with uncharacteristic patience until Mason reported.

It was perhaps this conference that produced Mason's most famous bridge—supposed to have been thrown across the Chickahominy during the Seven Days battles. Jackson explained the need for a long bridge to move the troops against the enemy.

"How long would it take, Mason?"

"General, give me two hundred men, and I'll have you over in twenty-four hours."

Jackson ordered his staff engineers to draw plans, assigned the troops to Mason, and left the front. Stonewall found the bridge complete the next day, on schedule to the hour.

"Your bridge is ready, General," Mason said. "But the plans haven't come yet."

It was Mason who is said to have saved Jackson's army from detection on a dangerous night march. Since Stonewall had a number of mules hauling his wagons, he feared that the animals would bray as they approached the nearby Federal camp. He called for Mason's advice, and was not disappointed:

"General, give me a few hanks of strong cord and about fifty men, and I'll have your mules quiet in an hour."

While the troops gaped at the spectacle, Mason's muleteers looped the cord around each mule's body in front of the hind legs, and tied down the tails of the animals.

"Mule never brays until he lifts his tail, General," Mason reported—and the army was off on a silent march.

There is a legend that Pickett's Charge at Gettysburg was twice enacted, the final scene contributing a fearful, if lesser, carnage to the traditions of that great battle.

During a Blue and Gray reunion on the field, so some have it, aging Confederates fell into ranks and walked across the broad terrain where Pickett's men had charged on July 3, 1863. The watching ancients in blue could not long remain bystanders, and as the feeble ranks moved up the slope toward the spot where once the angled stone wall had run, and where a clump of trees stood on Cemetery Ridge, there were Yankee yells:

"Come on, boys! By God, they never made it then—and they'll not do it now."

Upon which the old boys of the Grand Army of the Republic are alleged to have run into position along the ridge, and when the Confederate veterans hobbled up, to have sprung upon them tooth and nail, the whole mass tangling in a fierce scrap until officials managed to part them.

The enduring nickname of Stonewall Jackson is classed as a bit of folklore by some historians, who point out that no proof exists that the famed *nom du guerre* was actually applied by General Barnard Bee, the South Carolinian who died at First Manassas, soon after rallying his troops with the alleged cry: "Look, there stands Jackson like a stone wall!"

In rebuttal, a South Carolina tradition insists that Bee did utter those words—but that he was excoriating Jackson for his failure to launch a charge with his troops, rather than hold them in position on his hillside.

A bit of Missouri folklore, some of it embalmed in the Official Records, deals with the gallant death of the Confederate Colonel, Frisby H. McCullough, a cavalry leader engaged in the bitter guerrilla fighting in that state.

After a skirmish at Edina, in August, 1862, McCullough, who was ill, remained behind his troops, declining the offer of a body guard. Federals caught him hiding, in Confederate uniform, and a court-martial sentenced him to death on a charge of bushwhacking.

McCullough called for a brief respite to write his wife a

final letter—and was given fifteen minutes. The Colonel scratched out one sentence as he leaned against a wall, and pronounced himself ready for the execution.

By tradition, he asked that he be allowed to give the firing squad the signal for his death, and dropped a handkerchief which brought on the fatal volley. He lived for a few minutes, and as Federals bent over him, McCullough said, "May God forgive you for this cold-blooded murder."

Some latter-day tales of the war are a match for any of their predecessors. One concerning the fate of Stonewall Jackson is told by Roy A. Wykoff, Jr., of Davenport, Iowa:

In 1935 a retired army major, John Murphy, revealed to Wykoff that Stonewall Jackson was not killed at Chancellorsville, Virginia, in May, 1863, as his contemporaries and history would have it.

Murphy declared that as a Confederate sergeant he had served as orderly to Jackson, and as proof displayed a silver watch engraved: "To T.J. Jackson from Robert E. Lee."

Murphy's tale:

"Stonewall Jackson and I deserted from the Confederate States Army on May 2, 1863 at 9 P.M. We rode up the Plank Road to the Mountain, or Mineral Springs, Road, at Chancellorsville, and crossed the Union lines there.

"Eventually we rode to Gettysburg, Pennsylvania, where we found a group of dead Federal soldiers. This was in July, 1863. General Jackson put on a Federal soldier's uniform and found in its pocket papers identifying its owner as Moses E. Milner, California Volunteers.

"General Jackson joined the 1st U.S. Sharpshooters at Gettysburg, the regiment under Colonel Hiram Berdan.

"In 1867–68, General Jackson was a scout for General Custer—and served also under the name of 'California Joe' Milner in the Black Hills for General Crook.

"In 1876, this man (General Stonewall Jackson, alias 'California Joe' Milner) was shot from ambush near Fort Robinson, Nebraska, by two cattle rustlers.

"On November 1, as a lieutenant of the 14th U.S. Infantry,

I buried this man, Jackson-Milner, in a lead-sheathed coffin at Fort Robinson military cemetery."

As evidence, offered in face of the testimony of hundreds who saw Stonewall in his casket before his Richmond burial in May, 1863, Wykoff cites the records from Fort McPherson National Cemetery at Maxwell, Nebraska, where a grave numbered 5921, Section S, is occupied by Moses E. Milner. Officials confirm the record of Milner's burial, but know nothing of the legend itself.

A tale even more challenging to the imagination was offered Southern newspaper readers in 1958, by a Vienna correspondent signing himself simply as "C.R. Johnson." Late in the war, by this story, the Confederacy launched a two-stage rocket from near Richmond, aiming at Washington, about one hundred miles away.

This extraordinary missile was made possible by the work of a secret agent in England, who persuaded Lord Kelvin to liquefy oxygen (in advance of its accepted date of development), and enlisted the aid of the great German physicist, Ernst Mach, who contributed a small turbine and a gyroscopic stabilizer. With British-built machinery for liquefying oxygen and Mach's turbine, Confederate experts went to work in a shed on the banks of the James River.

A deep hole in the riverbank was fitted with a tube made of dismembered barrels of naval guns. The celebrated Matthew Fontaine Maury, father of modern navigation, calculated the trajectory.

The rocket itself was to get its original thrust from gun-cotton fired at the bottom of the tube, and was made at the huge Tredegar Iron Works in Richmond. The missile was trundled through Richmond's streets to the launching site in early March, 1865. Men from the Torpedo Bureau worked around the clock to prepare the rocket; a steam pipe was fed into the launching tube to provide power for the stabilizing vanes.

The missile arrived with the letters CSA cut in its nose cone, and President Davis and other officials added their names before the firing.

A network of scouts was spread in the country between Richmond and Washington as crude tracking station outposts, and when the rocket was fired by an electrical switch, men with telescopes saw it roar skyward, lose its first stage, and disappear from sight. The first stage, by this account, was recovered and returned to the torpedo shed.

A mystery developed: No eye saw the rocket come down, and since record books were destroyed with the fall of Richmond, the rocket's fate was unknown. The son of the Confederate agent in England, according to this folklorist or prankster, is now in his nineties, and does not wish to be disturbed by publicity which would attend his producing the authentic records of this event. His will, it is said, provides that these be made public.

Meanwhile, a fascinated audience ponders the fantastic prospect: Is there, somewhere in space, a veteran of almost one hundred years as an orbiting satellite, a missile bearing the outmoded initials: CSA?

Bibliography

AMONG the more general works of especial help in assembling this book were those of Douglas S. Freeman, Bruce Catton, Margaret Leech, Bell I. Wiley, Clifford Dowdey, Jay Monaghan, Clement Eaton, Robert Selph Henry, Shelby Foote, and Carl Sandburg.

Invaluable for revelations of little-known facts and tales of the war were a number of special studies, including these:

Allison, Guy, *Man's Most Valuable Words: The Gettysburg Address.* Gettysburg, 1956.

Baker, Lafayette, *History of the U.S. Secret Service.* Philadelphia, L.C. Baker, 1867.

Barron, S.B., *The Lone Star Defenders.* New York, Neale Publishing Co., 1908.

Bigelow, John, *France and the Confederate Navy.* New York, Harper & Brothers, 1888.

Bruce, Robert V., *Lincoln and the Tools of War.* Indianapolis, Bobbs-Merrill, 1956.

Bulloch, James D., *The Secret Service of the Confederate States in Europe.* New York, T. Yoseloff, 1959.

Cadwallader, Sylvanus, *Three Years with Grant.* New York, Knopf, 1955.

de Chambrun, Charles Adolphe, *Impressions of Lincoln and the Civil War.* New York, Random House, 1952.

Crowley, R.O., "The Confederate Torpedo Service." *Century,* June, 1898.

Dietz, August, *The Postal Service of the Confederate States of America*. Richmond, Press of the Dietz Printing Company, 1929.

Durkin, Joseph Thomas, *Stephen A. Mallory*. Chapel Hill, N.C., University of North Carolina Press, 1954.

Edmonds, George, *Facts and Falsehoods Concerning the War on the South*. Memphis, A.R. Taylor & Co., 1904.

Harwell, Richard B., *Confederate Music*. Chapel Hill, University of North Carolina Press, 1950.

Hawn, William, *All Around the Civil War; or Before and After*. New York, Wynkoop Hallenbeck Crawford Co., 1908.

Haydon, Frederick S., *Aeronautics in the Union and Confederate Armies*. Baltimore, The Johns Hopkins Press, 1941.

Livermore, Thomas L., *Numbers and Losses in the Civil War*. Boston, Houghton, Mifflin & Co., 1900.

Lonn, Ella, *Foreigners in the Confederacy*. Chapel Hill, University of North Carolina Press, 1940.

Love, William D., *Wisconsin in the War of the Rebellion*. Chicago, 1866.

McCartney, Clarence E., *Highways and Byways of the Civil War*. Pittsburgh, 1938.

McGuire, Hunter, and Christian, George L., *The Confederate Cause and Conduct in the War Between the States*. Richmond, 1907.

Orton, Richard H., *Records of California Men in the War of the Rebellion*. Sacramento, J.D. Young, 1890.

Phisterer, Frederick, *Statistical Record of the Armies of the United States*. New York, C. Scribner's Sons, 1886.

Rains, George W., *History of the Confederate Powder Works*. Augusta, Ga., *Chronicle and Constitutionalist*, 1882.

Rauscher, Frank, *Music on the March*. Philadelphia, W.F. Fell, 1892.

Slabaugh, Arlie R., *Confederate States Paper Money*. Racine, 1958.

Smith, Edward C., *The Borderland in the Civil War*. New York, The Macmillan Co., 1927.

Tunnard, W.H., *A Southern Record: The History of the Third Regiment, Louisiana Infantry*. Baton Rouge, 1866.

Vandiver, Frank, *Ploughshares Into Sword: Josiah Gorgas and Confederate Ordnance*. Austin, Texas, University of Texas Press, 1952.

Of particular interest was the Annie Jones file, Civil War Search Room, National Archives, Washington, D.C.

An army newspaper, *The Free South*, published in Beaufort, S.C., by Federal troops was of value in its issue of June 13, 1863: Vol. 1, No. 23.